BECAUSE WE HAVE ALL LIVED HERE

April 1/19

To Aley...

To prayerful journeys and continuing inspiration.
All good things,

Peter Hordy

Because We Have All Lived Here

Poems from the South Shore
A Group of Seven Poets

Edited by John B. Lee

Copyright © Black Moss Press, 2017

All rights reserved. No part of this publication may be reproduced or transmitted in any form by any means, electronic or mechanical, including photocopying, recording, or any information storage and retrieval system, without permission in writing from the publisher or a licence from The Canadian Copyright Licencing Agency (Access Copyright). For an Access Copyright licence, visit www.accesscopyrights.ca or call toll free 1.800.893.5777.

Library and Archives Canada Cataloguing in Publication

Because we have all lived here : poems from the South Shore / a group of seven poets.

Edited by John B. Lee.
Poems by Carlinda D'Alimonte, Marty Gervais, Peter Hrastovec, D.A. Lockhart, Dorothy Mahoney, Mary Ann Mulhern, and Vanessa Shields.

ISBN 978-0-88753-584-0 (softcover)

    1. Windsor Region (Ont.)—Poetry. 2. Canadian poetry (English)—Ontario—Windsor. 3. Canadian poetry (English)—21st century. I. Lee, John B., 1951-, editor

PS8295.7.W553B43 2017   C811'.6080971332   C2017-903346-8

Cover Image: Used with permission from the Windsor Community Museum
Cover Design: Katrina Hesman
Book Design: Karen Veryle Monck

 Published by Black Moss Press at 2450 Byng Road, Windsor, Ontario, N8W 3E8. Canada. Black Moss books are distributed in Canada and the U.S. by Fitzhenry & Whiteside, 195 Allstate Parkway, Markham, ON, L3R 4T8. All orders should be directed there.

The City of Windsor's Celebrating2017 Initiative is funded [in part] by the Government of Canada, Ontario150, and the City of Windsor. L'initiative Celebrating2017 est financée [en partie] par le gouvernement du Canada, le programme Ontario150, et la Ville de Windsor.

Black Moss would like to acknowledge the generous financial support from both the Canada Council for the Arts and the Ontario Arts Council.

 Canada Council for the Arts Conseil des Arts du Canada

PRINTED IN CANADA

Contents

What Poets Might Make of a City. 9

This is a City 11

Marty Gervais

The Original Five Towns:
Confederation Day, July 1, 1867: Windsor 15
From the Third Floor of the Duff-Baby House
Sandwich Ontario. 17
The Last of the Passenger Pigeons of Our Lady of Assumption . . 19
Cathedrals. 21
Mr. McLuhan and the Windsor Cow 23
The Old Stables at Kenilworth Race Track. 25
Remembering the Great Walkerville Race of 1896 27
Sleeping Car. 30
Armed Stage Coach Chatham to Sandwich 1827 32
That Day in Sandwich with the Prime Minister 34
Planting Pear Trees 36
Dance with the Devil 37
Schiller's Bush. 40
Tom Yawkey. 42

D.A. Lockhart

Our Songs Reflect that which has Passed 47
Louis Gervais Carves into this Turtle Shell Earth 48
Two Dead Men of Chatham. 49
Last Chief of these Straits 50
Mimegwesi Shall Release Them from the Shore 51
This Sanctuary Shall Carry Forth our Songs. 52
John Prince Drew a Line that Ends in Essex. 53
Through the Dull Him that May Never End 54
Our Constellation that Divides Us 55
In the War Room 56
Neon Shall Make This Night Electric 58

Carlinda D'Alimonte

Windsor 61
Seven Sisters 62
Holy Discourse 65
Crossing the River 68
Because We Have Lived Here 71
Could It Be the Same City 74
Who We Were and What We Could Do 75
My Father Outside the Chrysler Assembly Plant, 1955 78
In a Downtown Windsor Restaurant 81

Peter Hrastovec

Walkerville Reflections 85
Heppenstall's 86
Land-Castered 88
Number One Navajo 90
A Stable Influence 93
Tools 95
Movements 98
Emily Carr Hangs in a Gallery 100
Anti-Theatre 102
Open Sore 104
Shaughnessy's Gone to Pelee 108

Dorothy Mahoney

Ford City 113
Searching for Jesus 114
Sand 116
Border City Boxing 117
Down the Road 118
The Memory of Water 119
Passing Time 120
Generations 121

Mary Ann Mulhern

Riverside 125
Curse of Peche Island 128
Ruins of a Mansion 129
Peaches from the River 130
To Keep a Distance 131
Child of Glengarda 132
Bones of Glengarda 133
Playboy at Glengarda 134
To Keep Vigil 135
St. Ursula's Sculptor 136
Abars 137
An Inn of Prohibition 138
Blessing of Riverside 139
The Taste Tells 140
Brides of MacKenzie Hall 141

Vanessa Shields

Reflections on Being a Poet in the City of Windsor 145
Double-Sessions at Wheels Roller Rink 146
I Want to Know What Love Is 148
Drive in to Movie Madness 150
One Love 151
Cluster 153
Man O'War 155
Tornado 158
Some Find Hands: Walker Farms, January 1894 163
The Day the Fire Blazed: Walker Farms, 1937 166
One Lot—The Voice of What Remains of Walker Farms 168
A Mootual Moostake 169
The Canadian Dream 171

Because I Haven't Lived Here: an outsider's view 173

Carlinda D'Alimonte, Marty Gervais, Vanessa Shields

D.A. Lockhart, Peter Hrastovec

What Poets Might Make of a City

John B. Lee   Poet Laureate of the city of Brantford in perpetuity Poet Laureate of Norfolk County for life

Canada has produced her urban poets. Archibald Lampman gave us a glimpse of a dystopian future in his nineteenth century poem, "The City of the End of Things." Dennis Lee immortalized Toronto in his masterful *Civil Elegies*. And so, Windsor's Poet Laureate Marty Gervais put out the call and the muses answered and the city came alive. The past must be grateful to be remembered well, and the future beholden to those who preserve the present. In *Because We Have All Lived Here* the reader might join these poets in honouring the five towns on the south shore of the Detroit River as it flows from Lake St. Clair to Lake Erie, or as we read from Sandwich through Riverside, the compass of our consciousness traveling west by northwest and then south to the newest environs of the vibrant border city Windsor, the jewel of Souwesto.

What meaning might poets make of a city when the city in question is home? And what of the group of seven poets from Windsor who combine their individual voices into a chorus in this study of belonging. In the ancient tradition of singers and bards of every civilization since the time of Gilgamesh, through Homer's Troy, to Virgil's Rome, to Blake's London, poets have lived in cities and given those cities in which they have dwelt the gift of their studied attention. Whether it be a contemplation of the recent past of their own formative years, or the distant past in time before time with the city unborn from the wilderness, or the less distant past when the record of human habitation built what remains through generations from when the founders first imagined her skyline or the grid of her streets to when that skyline changed and the ghost of her structures haunt the memory of those who remember and of those who imagine.

And though we may think of Athens or Paris or of any of the great cities of the world as worthy of immortality, and though we may request and require a famous destination like Beijing, or Moscow, or Berlin, or we may crave the architectural wonders of new world like those erected on the magnificent mile of Chicago, or as it is with the towering forest of Manhattan high rises, if we live where we live and we are where we are as attentive and fully awake and alive, then this too might be a place of places. It is the life of the city that gives life to the writing, as it is the quality of the writing that gives life to the city.

Mary Ann Mulhern, Dorothy Mahoney, Carlinda D'Alimonte

This Is A City

This is a city that won't leave me
To define it is to steal its laboured breath

This is a city that breaks my heart
To love it is to hate its existence

This is a city that wounds the land
To serve it is to break its tender back

This is a city that refuses to die
To heal it is to strengthen its disease

This is a city that I call home
To call it anything else is a lie

This is a city that loves to give
To shun it is to feed the fuel

This is a city that will not be understood
To teach it is to warp its history

This is a city I cannot leave
To define me is to force me to go

Vanessa Shields

Marty Gervais

Marty Gervais, Windsor's first poet laureate, is an award-winning poet, journalist and photographer. His book *The Rumunners* was a Canadian bestseller. He teaches English and journalism at the University of Windsor.

The Original Five Towns

Confederation Day, July 1, 1867: Windsor

There were speeches and 21-gun salutes
and parades and games and
there was drinking—

an effigy of Charles Tupper
burned at Halifax Harbour
alongside a live rat

a roasted ox to feed the poor
at the foot of Toronto's Church Street

and later that night a sky alight
with fireworks over Queen's Park

and a Hamilton girl writing
about a sky full of shooting stars
a fountain of red and green and blue
and a father promising her
she was a very lucky girl
to be a child in Canada today

But here in this river town
with its muddy roads threading out
along a shoreline alive with revelers
and stilt-walkers and
clapboard storefronts draped
with the Union Jack

came redcoats with bayonets
scurrying from nearby barracks

not to celebrate or honor or applaud
but to face a rioting of angry men
who pelted them with rocks

By nightfall, the rioters
—defeated and sad—trundled home
while men and women, swinging lanterns
paraded home through darkened streets
marvelling at a ribbon of bonfires
lighting the curved south shore

Yet there still was no mistaking
this summer moon high above this river
turning away in shame
to behold how the streets below
heaved with lament
as club-wielding blacks and whites
marshalled in this new day

From the Third Floor of the Duff-Baby House Sandwich Ontario

I stand at a north window
on the third floor
of this stately house
imagine families
crossing the river in winter cold
hauling supplies
loaded up on sleds

refugees of war
desperate for shelter, food, warmth

seeking that one thin horizontal line
of eerie silence stretched
across a flat sky—
courthouse, church steeple, graveyard

hear curses and laughter
in the icy British stillness

I imagine soldiers dining here
in frivolous candlelight
fretting over a morning assault
fearing traitors and spies and assassins
feeling spooked by a cold January moon

From this third floor
I imagine men and women and children
slipping across a windswept river

with daytime collapsing all around
yet somehow lifting themselves
despite this meddlesome burden of fear

Then suddenly I wake from my reverie
to the carpenters
hammering down the roof
from a cannonball
that crashed through
in a battle that won nothing
for nobody

The Last of the Passenger Pigeons of Our Lady of Assumption

The Black Robes are gone
So are the villagers, farmers and soldiers
I have nothing more to say

Yet my wings carry me across
the morning river—
steeples of St. Anne's rising in the mist
signaling to me
like the Holy Shepherd's hand
I wonder about my brothers & sisters
there roosting under the eaves
away from the coming rain
voices silenced

I have nothing more to say

Yet I see the turmoil among men & women
struggles of war, of famine, of typhoid
hunger and fear

I have nothing more to say

Yet my eyes are clear
as I drift high above
a sprawling lazy river
trace the comings and goings
of a people forgotten now
in the chaos of deafening cannons
and bloody skirmishes
and scars of political wranglings

I have nothing more to say—
my ears exploding with the *Angelus*

I am close to heaven
I am a ghost of what was
and I am silent

sailing in the moody-gray day
my wings lifting with the weight of history
my head bursting with philosophies
my tongue alive with language

I have nothing to more to say
I see, and I am mute
I sail and I am silent

I have a voice that may sing
soaring high about the steeple's mysteries
That define the pure frailty of God

And now I rise above generations
and float above
the miraculous blue of this sleeping river

believing in nothing more than
than one final single flight that signals
the end of a long day

when there's no reason to speak

I see, and I am mute
I sail and I am silent

Cathedrals

They were cathedrals
—these sprawling factories
with frosted glass metal-framed windows
that tilted open to a landscape
of wartime houses and brick schools
—the men, like monks, moved
in slow motion, and my father
in a white shirt and crooked bowtie
paced among them
worried over meeting the numbers
Today, these places lie mute—
edifices of crumbling brick
cracked and broken windows
and the rubble-strewn earth
taking back the 20th century
with trees bursting up
through the busted concrete
Months before my father died
we cruised the empty streets
and picked our way among the ruins
of the old Studebaker and Ford plants
the Motor Lamp on Seminole,
boarded up dry goods stores
and barber shops and fish & chip joints
We stood in the middle of the sunlit floor
of the place where he made headlamps—
an acre of concrete once complicated
by conveyor belts and sturdy steel columns
and he told me of those mornings

walking to work from Albert Road
chomping on an apple
a metal lunch pail tucked under his arm
a skinny boy of sixteen having landed here
from the mining towns in the north
a job on the line, a job he'd never quit
till his heart gave out, and now
there are mornings when I pause
before a single building
and peer through a toothless wall
of broken glass imagining life
on that concrete floor
He told me once how he'd trade
everything to return to that time
that sweet independence
of youth and a job
and a cheque on Fridays

Mr. McLuhan and the Windsor Cow

Maybe this is what McLuhan thought
when he happened upon
this daydreaming cow
as she trotted
with reckless abandon into
that country road

What was she doing
when there was
nothing else to do?

Conjuring better pastures
maybe ruminating
about meandering into a nearby parking lot
among open car windows
hoping for a spot
to snoop and maybe snooze
under a blue Windsor sky

picturing what it might be like
to slip into the back seat
of an old Chevrolet
and doze away the day

There's nothing to do as usual
so why not wander
weary of all that cow inertia
and step out from the others
and leave behind

their annoying bovine gossip
in the lazy humid air

maybe step aside from
that tired list of silly names
Mr. Farmer has christened them:
Devilish Delilah, Crafty Caroline
Pain-in-the-Arse Mary-Rose
and *Ooola-la Ola*

There's nothing to do as usual
so why not wander
where the grass is greener

and why not move gracefully
past the open gate
into that ribbon of road
and break free of the regime
of every day

and finally be the girl you always
imagined on those tiresome
going-nowhere days

abandoning cow passivity
to leave behind a staring crowd

The Old Stables at Kenilworth Race Track

That day driving out
to the tumbledown stables
south of the city
I knew nothing of that moment in October 1920
I'd gone there with a woman I'd met at a bookstore
—horseback riding late, late afternoon
straw and dust and manure
the sharp odour of Absorbine
and tobacco and seeing
threadbare plaid blankets folded over
the gates in the horse barn
and the final rays of sunlight
pouring into the stalls

I watched this quiet elderly man leading the horses
out to the yard, the rich chestnut slope of their beauty
accentuated by late-fall light
I knew nothing of that moment so long ago
but think of it now, too late,
and realize this man was there—
a boy among the stables
fetching straw and oats
his milky blue eyes and boyish hands
guiding the horses
into the silent moonlit yard at dawn

I want him to be there again with the great ones
—the race of the century
Man O'War and *Sir Barton*

I want him to be at edges, slipping past
with pails of clean water
to sense the stillness of the stall
where motionless Man O'War stood
—they say Big Red, as he was called,
was so beautiful it made you want to cry
his very stillness, that
of a coiled spring, a crouched tiger

I want to believe Big Red scared the boy
that first morning in the fall
Yet I knew nothing of that day in October
when I drove out to those old stables
where this boy once stood in awe
of men who kept watch over the great stallion
I knew nothing of the track we rode on
at twilight where Big Red once galloped
like a nightmare roaring into history
I wished now I had paid attention
I wished I had remembered what
this man looked like, what he might've said
I wished now we could've talked
Instead, I sat perched on a broken-down horse
trotting along a track I knew nothing about
trailing after a new girlfriend
thinking only of her
and my next move

Remembering the Great Walkerville Race of 1896

I figured my 70th birthday
would get me a bicycle

but that never happened
and why would it

I get no exercise at all
no longer bothering
to make excuses about
avoiding the gym

I promise nothing
not even for the after life

I stare at my naked body
in the bathroom mirror
after a hot bath—
a slight paunch

no longer speculating
if anyone might desire this
pale solitary figure

but the bicycle—
I thought I might get one

believed someone might
get the idea

see me ride
through morning streets
overhear the sudden kitchen clatter
through open windows
and screen doors

catch the bewildering whiff of perfume
as in a driveway
a young woman swings open
the door of her car

but then conjure up
the famous 10-mile bicycle race
of Charlie Fox that late afternoon
of August 1st. 1896

wily competitors lined up
at Walker Road
in front of the planing mill
gentlemen in straw hats
women in long skirts
clouds scattered over
a skyline that earlier
seemed angry and glum
leaving the roads
soggy and rutted

as the riders made their way
south along Walker Road
toward Tecumseh

the prize that day
a gold Waltham watch

I imagine Charlie fighting
brisk head winds eventually
taking the lead
and winning the pocket watch
that he would keep all his life

then joining with his buddies
for Stephen Foster songs
and day-cold beer

and there I am reliving
that moment—my bicycle
journeying past boundaries
beyond the expected

I can see Charlie Fox
just ahead of me—
my legs straining for victory
yet the wind telling me
to give up

And I am brought back
to *this* moment—where instead
I am pausing naked in the mirror
running a hand over my bald head
turning to my right
and taking a good look

now I fancy the journey alone
departing red-brick neighbourhoods
that rouse in the early hours

And I *am* happy with this

Sleeping Car

I walk over it every day

I cross broken pavement in a garage
cluttered with waste bins, lacrosse sticks
garden tools, hockey equipment,
paint tins, flaccid bicycle tires

every day

a car that sleeps below the floor
—A Ford Model A, the automobile
that put the world on wheels

every day

imagine scrambling into its cramped
covert frame, peering out
its tiny flat window
more like a flat screen TV

marveling at its interior simplicity:
steering wheel, 3 pedals
on the floor, hand brake

but the pedals are spaced differently,
one soley for reverse

There's also an adjustment
for spark plugs and a throttle

I walk over it

All l I can do is will its life
back into place

slip out the choke
adjacent to the right fender,
engage the crank lever under the rad
slowly turn it clockwise to prime
then hop into the car
insert the ignition key
twist the setting to magneto
adjust the the timing stalk upward
move the throttle stalk downward

then return to the front of the car
and crank the lever to start

Someone once said
the layout of throttle, brake and shifter
made driving a Model T
archaic and dangerous
—like dancing the Charleston
while loading a musket after a big night
at a speak-easy

every day

imagine the day it was placed there
when they assembled this garage
dumping the car into the empty cavity
before heaping soil all around its
boxy black build

I walk over it every day

a car that sleeps below my feet
buried beneath a world
that has leapt ahead of itself

Armed Stage Coach Chatham to Sandwich 1827

I can see them now—
laying down the law
so the Border Cities
got their mail—

these members
of the Chatham Vigilante Society
each paying $1 for protection
to help slip the Royal Mail through

I can see them now—
these armed stage coaches
with agents, rifle ready, austere
and surveilling the perilous route
wending their way along
muddy bumpy Indian trails
running along the river road
to Windsor and Sandwich

I can see them now—
these agency men smug
and suspicious, high up, rocking
back and forth in drafty carriages
or in winter huddled around
a cramped wooden stove inside
as the horses struggled
to haul these wagons along the river
to the Border Cities

I can see them now—
these lumbering rickety wagons
of graceless four-horse stage coaches
risking the menace of robbery
along stump-dotted roadways

I can see them now—
these bearded armed men inside
their mesmeric eyes tracing the horizon
of river and lake and and line of trees beyond
hands ready to battle

That Day in Sandwich with the Prime Minister

His voice a singsong normally
whole sentences drifting out
and rising and falling
but forever lost in a monotone
as he paced back and forth
before the crowd
scowling at his opponent

Today in Sandwich
Sir John A is silent
and seated, smug and
staring at the stage floor
in this open-air debate
a drunken stupor clouding
Mackenzie's reasoned jargon
ripping into him
scandal and hearsay
and political wrangle

Sir John A slumps in a chair
lingering for that moment
to lift his frumpy but narrow frame
to tower before the crowd

and warily waves a crooked finger
all the while struggling
to retrieve the right word
in this scandal and hearsay
and political wrangle

then suddenly
vomits over the stage

An abrupt hush

and Sir John A's left hand
almost in slow motion
reaches for a handkerchief
tucked deep within
the pockets of his waist coat
then swabs his mouth

and eyes agape

he begins his apology
and turns to his opponent
and with a polite and civil nod of his head
he says, "Mr. Chairman,
I don't know how it is
but every time I hear
the Honorable Gentleman speak
it turns my stomach!"

Planting Pear Trees

The Black Robes arrived in late spring
long sprawling canoes
hugging the bend in the river

till they spotted men and women
waving from the south bank

and came ashore bearing gifts
and pear tree seedlings from France

The Fathers planted the trees
in groups of twelve—

setting only one apart like the apostle

All these years later
one survives in a field by
the mouth of the river

solitary exile
its tired branches drooping
stretching for repose in the black soil

planted there 300 years ago
to bear fruit, to bear truth

Dance with the Devil

Dance with the devil
—sooner or later
you'll pay the price

says a boxing coach
who had trained the three boys
in London, Ontario

—sons living in the shadow
of the man who in one gloomy week
in January 1977, right before the snow began,
killed union boss Charlie Brooks

and the boys in reckless grace
patterned the steps of a father
—one, gunned down in a house in London
another, in a street in Calgary
a third, by his own hand

Dancing with the price
and paying devil

All three paid for the distant memory
of the assassin who kicked down
a door at the union hall
on Turner Road and unloaded
a .44 calibre rifle
into the startled gaze
of the union boss

dancing with the price
and paying the devil

And those sons watched on television
as 8,000 CAW workers filed into the icy wintry streets
to march in a hushed border town—
heads bowed in the cold
silently mourning the man everyone called a hero

meanwhile saw their father
shunted off to courtrooms
and treatment centres
declaring himself insane,
not-guilty of killing a champion

Years later the boys learned
to move like lightning—sleuths
with jabs and uppercuts and right hooks
slipping and swaying
in late afternoon gyms
dancing and sparring with history
moving into corners
into shadows, into
remembrance that demands payback

and their ol' man never failed
to wend his way down to the gym
having his freedom,
having never spent
a day in jail for killing Brooks

and the ol' man leaned heavy
on the ropes of the ring
exhorting his boys to rip on their assailants

to dance with the devil
and forget about the price

and it was there in the arms
of his sons' coach that he died
felled by a failing heart

dancing with the price
and paying the devil

No longer yearning to toy
with headlines that called him a monster,

He had already danced with the devil

Schiller's Bush

Voices in the street frightened me
I was six
I could hear shouting
horns, laughter, foot stomping, singing
The next morning at breakfast
my father was smiling and poking at us
asking if we had overheard the revellers
It was New Year's Day, 1952
my first memories of Riverside Ontario

Or maybe it was the way we called on friends
at their homes
first thing in the morning
We'd race up the three-step
concrete block porches of brick war time houses
crane our necks
to an upstairs bedroom window
bellow out
in the cold morning air
our friend's name.

If you took a moment
to scan the neighbourhood houses
along the street
you'd see this repeated at other doorsteps
—boys standing and shouting out names.

Moments later
we'd hear and see our friends emerge

usually madly fighting a jacket
around their shoulders
and off we'd sprint
to a nearby ball diamond
or south to the railway tracks
that we'd follow east to "Schiller's Bush"
Back then, it was a rich forest
where we'd build bonfires
and roast frozen weenies skewered on coat hangers
and dream of being *courier-de-bois*
Today, traces of that original bush
still exist along Tranby, nearer to Lauzon
Homes now stand where we once played
Today I'm 70, and I make my way by car
to sit in a tiny room
waiting for my doctor
to ask me to drop my drawers
and bend over
—time to check my prostate
as though hearing only my own voice
I pretend all over again
I'm running wildly through the woods

Tom Yawkey

You might never guess
this was home for Tom Yawkey
—the square-jawed owner
of the Red Sox

and how each July
he'd return to perch nearby
on a flipped over beer crate
still wearing a wide-brimmed felt fedora
grinning at his ballplayers
now mere fleeting shadows
in the July dusk

You might never hear that single brassy wail
of a trumpet
rising in the dusk
as others in a hired Dixieland band
improvised and toyed
and harmonized

This was home away from home
for the square-jawed owner
of the Red Sox, a moment
to remember his grandfather
who once owned this fist of forest land
that lengthened like an open palm
down to the river

and every time the team
played Detroit, the fatigued ballplayers
rode the tumbledown bus
out of Windsor to its open fields

there waiting for a collection of chairs
rows of picnic tables, and beer
and women, and this Dixieland band
and a make-shift ball diamond

Tom would settle down and eye
his swarthy ballplayers
study how they moved lazily
with the grace of precision —
their laughter punctuating
the summer air
their eager hands reaching for beer
or catching the sleek curves
of nearby women friends

Soon Tom could be seen
forking over a fistful of bills
to the black musicians from Detroit
to continue that moment
across this open sandlot field
to keep the pace alive
keep those ballplayers' weary legs dancing

Slumped there on a beer crate,
Tom would review
how his men paid no notice

to the approaching night
as it fluttered over
blanketing the slumbering field
and its dusty baselines
strewn with empty lifeless mitts
and baseball bats

Instead the men howled madly
at the moon that roused awake
in the darkness
above the trees and far
from the sound of the river
to the north
or the bebop beat

Instead the men circled the baselines
chasing ghosts of the chalk dust
fearing nothing of the moment
except the sharp eye of their owner
who rested nearby —
a fedora cocked to one side
steady eyes settling on their future

You might never guess that the faint sound
among fallen trees and gurgling creeks
is a band of black musicians
their music bouncing in the still night
far far below a reconciling sky
that frowns woefully
like a forgotten fan
no longer knowing whom to cheer

D.A. Lockhart

D.A. Lockhart is the author of *This City at the Crossroads* (Black Moss Press 2017) and *Big Medicine Comes to Erie* (Black Moss Press 2016). His work has appeared in numerous journals including the *Malahat Review, Hawai'i Review, OSU's The Journal, The Windsor Review,* and *Contemporary Verse 2*. Lockhart is a graduate of the Indiana University-Bloomington MFA in Creative Writing program. He is a member of the Moravian of the Thames First Nation that lives on Odawa land that is now occupied by the Pillette Village neighbourhood.

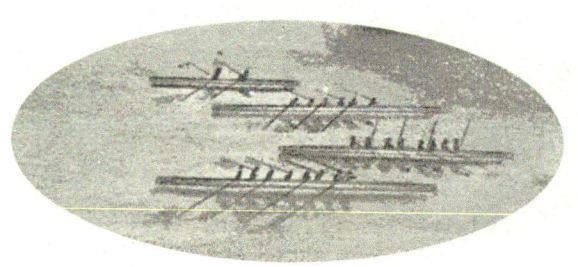

Our Songs Reflect that which has Passed

Sandwich, home to Hurons, Catholic Missionaries, men of industry, proud survivors of American slavery, countless others, has many songs. Each of them is a critical part of the fabric of our origins, the meshwork of our city, the foundation for our region. Roots are important. We must know them to understand who it is we are and what we must become. Songs bring us to those roots, let us feel something beyond the dry text of historic plaques and passages in glossy-paged history books. Know that my roots run deep in the earth of Turtle Island. I am turtle clan of the Lenape Nation through my father's people. My mother's people have roots that stretch back to the first European arrivals to Amherstburg and Harrow, embracing their connection to the great mother in both French and English. All of them working people, people who understood the rhythms of the land. We came to the land that Windsor now rests upon after it had been walked upon for countless generations by others. We learned their songs, our songs merged with theirs, this land became ours too. Our memories and the songs that carry them forward to the next generations speak to the manner of where we have come from, construct the framework by which we measure our place.

Louis Gervais Carves into this Turtle Shell Earth

Here, our turtle shell was carved by plow,
made mirror the claw marks of mishibizhiw
so that Upper Canada could declare dominion.
Each turn of plow, breaking the quiet of fires
from nearby Huron homes, proclaiming the will
to look south, towards untamed stars swirling
above Erie. From here, wind-blown waves pound
upstream with the tacit cruelty colonists
spare for wildlife, those that follow their wake,
and to quiet the manner land shows will. Alongside
upturned earth a steady rivulet of a creek runs
inland and vanishes like the names bestowed upon
sacred bloodlines, no record nor map traces the passing
of, only whispers aghast at raw furrowed earth.

Two Dead Men of Chatham

Well past the purples and incense of vespers
they were certain to have seen a white horse
upon the crest of Mill Street as it rose above
the docks and channels cut to shore. Perhaps,
a glimpse, although surely it lingered beneath
the two dead men, awash in chimney smoke,
and the quiet complaints about the dignity
of iron cages. Lot four, East Russell Street
two corpses left to punish this town with fear
that murder shall come only by the Crown's hand
meet the cavil of mill paddles against an oil slick
sky and quiet of sleep by the thud of iron, wood,
and the dead returning to earth. Followed by the trot
of visitant into a night stretched well past prayer.

Last Chief of these Straits

Speak it, say the name into medicine ribbons
of smoke, say them into this industrial sky
like tobacco passed between grandfather,
the jingle dance curvature of cedar stands
and the sing-song of tallgrass. Call it down
from above, from Creator, let it descend
like an eagle feather against earth that now takes
no name for those that knew songs and carried
voices for which creation carved the land to form.
Chief Joseph White lies elsewhere, in earth sold
for a chance at personhood. The knowledge comes
that clan duties stop where songs succumb to loss.
In this place marked by surveyor grids, speak his name,
for what remains is eminent to that which sought to erase.

Mimegwesi Shall Release Them from the Shore

Beneath us, men have toiled pulling salt
from the veins of creation, men who knew
nothing of mapmakers or customs agents
and the lines they cut. Mist atop cascading
river and in morning sun what remains
unseen awaits what is due, that which rests
upon shore shall be released to the currents
in the river beyond this still air. Though men
still toil beneath us, the earth remains steady,
the air free of the crackles of kizzhik and semaa.
Cattails and tallgrass bob, bely the pathways
of mimegwesi as they swing to free errant branches,
used cups, and the foothold of those upon shore
that dare to take without that which is due.

This Sanctuary Shall Carry Forth our Songs
(for Sandwich First Baptism Church)

The want for carried freedom ends here.
Carried as it was through hushed exodus
nights, north star quilts, and the pursuit
of the drinkin' gourd, freedom manifests
itself into this brick crowned temple mount
along the back lots of a promise land.
Old man river a few blocks north and here
against the sweet revelations of light and dark,
this meagre church rises to greet elms tops
and the crisp northern bite of late autumn sky.
Know that struggles do not end, but change
and songs shall always sing us through. Go Down
Moses to that river and sing so every Pharaoh
shall know this people, our people have been let go.

John Prince Drew a Line that Ends in Essex

In you we are left cautious with bear trap
and spiked-fence rumours, a paranoid crust
revealed by the manner those with guilt
protect the firmament from those they thought
forever gone and the way age reveals myth.
Debts owed by fathers provide the reason
one flees to the hinterland. Scares of patriot
risings in the aftermath of rebellions churn public
law to private bloodlust and four dead men return
in the woodlot murk of a farmhouse on the edge
of town. With age myths hide men. Namesake
roadways through homesteads rendered quiet
politicians in the ways a Thomas Splitlog signature
can never erase people that knew none of your myths.

Through the Dull Hum that May Never End

Despite the moan that rises as if a little spirit
released a flatline purl, this grinding hum comes on
like bone-weary workers lured on by overtime
and the steadiness of hourly work, routine labour
in the magma cooked insides of an island sawed-off
by men from the slow-rising bedrock of shore. Backs
turned, the great medicine stone was shattered by Lasalle.
Restless still, ancestors stir amidst furnaces set loose
on ore and coke. Our ground hums and we bask
in white noise slurry while bulk carriers pass us
in a spilled mercury riverside night. Through it all
that toothache dull hum calls out in ceremony that
in all moments of creation stone, broken or not, holds
spirit that crimes ancient and modern cannot dissipate.

Our Constellation that Divides Us

The same fire that took Windsor turned gravel
to rail, whispers of automotive moguls buried
that rail beneath with grey asphalt inertia stretched
from gutter to gutter. From here we are left with
white walls grinding out a drone hum, mechanical
as if to replace the coarse coos of passenger pigeons.
Spirits whose chorus reminds us riverport cities
are built at will, not by the persistence of ancestors
Atop this willfully laid path you stare down
the Ambassador lying perpendicular to you, teal,
bathed in jaundiced light, it is our constellation
and conveys myths of the ways lines work against
the ways we wish to move. The lights and scaffolding
rise up and steal away paths taken before totemic fires.

In the War Room

Thursday night finds us with the clank
of half-full OV bottles, pungent smokies
on a five-roller grill, and the all too bold
declarations of what must done to break
the neutral zone trap. To be certain,
London was in town because voices rang out
with reservations, more akin to post-shift
prayers that follow factory work, cracked
knuckle tired, and are placed before
a constant God who is disinclined to break
the injustice of big men in distant cities
casting the toil of workers a lesser fate.

Here in this, the war room, between periods
bathed in mid-century teal covered walls, voices
echo as if in an Erie street basement rec room.
A propped open door drawing the damp cold
from Wyandotte, these rises and falls etching out
how to defend and counter each attack, to turn
back that which we believe scrappiness can deflect,
to overrun the indifference afford each of us
by unanswered prayers and blindfolded linesmen.

We delineate our pedigree from Pronovost
to Quenneville, Bowler to Ott, Downie to Hall,
we have faith that determined bluster and effort
shall turn the tide. Confirmed by our gospel
that Bulldogs inspired more fear than Spitfires
and that in a province given to ice, us standing

in the warmish shadows of Motown, long past
borders drawn further up the 401, our claim to heritage
is the manner in which we fight that which we aren't.

Two quick buzzers and we empty from here
to the bowl first run by Cougars and onto benches
and seats built for folks unfamiliar with NAFTA,
the declining middleclass, and hockey in the desert.
From puck drop to whistle every plan, every testimony
will rain down upon those foolish enough to skate
against this city at the start of the Great Queen's Highway.

Neon Shall Make This Night Electric

In the passing of the distant shower know
that the water rushing downgrade through
the rust-coloured concrete ditch beneath
the Curry Avenue bridge reflects
that proximity to events does not limit
the manner they act upon our world.

To the east, low shelves of cloud grasp
at oak and maple tree tops, mirror
the street level caustic sodium vapour light,
searching for the sing-songs and churls
that the great crescent marsh sang back
to passing fronts. Found now in a namesake
blacktop strip staring back, an unholy glare.

Crossing the back lip of that strip mall
parking lot, our night rises, two-car lengths
above the asphalt surface; neon in green,
yellow, a hint of thunderbird blue, bent
triangle at speed that declares in triumphant
tangerine that this is Yorktown Square
to the silent earth around and dark folds
as empty roadway gives way to this night
electric and is reflected in oily water archipelago.

Carlinda D'Alimonte

Carlinda D'Alimonte is author of two books of poetry published by Black Moss Press—*Now That We Know Who We Are* (2004), and *Other Living Things* (2009). Her poetry has appeared in *Contemporary Verse 2*, *The Missouri Review*, *The Windsor Review*, and many anthologies. D'Alimonte has taught high school English and Creative Writing for twenty-five years. Prior to her teaching high school, she worked as a sessional instructor and multi-media producer at the University of Windsor and a researcher and writer for CBC television. She lives in Tecumseh, Ontario.

Windsor

Being a part of this project has further heightened my pride in our community. I grew up in the Windsor area, attended and worked at the University of Windsor, taught in a number county and city high schools, and raised my family here. I know this city and county well, or at least I thought I knew it well. In undertaking to write these poems, I uncovered so much I didn't know. For example, I was inspired by the fascinating history of Hotel Dieu Hospital (where, by the way, I was born). I was filled with admiration for the Sisters of the Religious Hospitallers of Saint Joseph, an order that originated in France but had a large constituency in Quebec. I was also deeply touched by the courage and strength of character of some of our Black leaders in the community. Three of the poems I've written for this project deal with particularly strong, principled women, who donning their thick skins, worked hard despite great hardship, to improve life for the people of Windsor and Essex County.

Windsor is one of the most culturally diverse cities in the country. Many of us relate directly to the immigrant experience. I think this is why today we are so accommodating and welcoming to new Canadians. One of my poems relates to a very challenging experience of my father's in the 1955, the year I was born. Today, Italians do not experience the worst discrimination in our culture, but in the fifties and sixties, things were quite different and they did suffer significantly at the hands of the less sensitive members of the community. I think there are important messages in this: immigrants come in waves; each group has suffered in its own way; individuals fight back in their own ways. As a reulst, things change and often improve over time.

Seven Sisters

A Tribute to the Founding Sisters of Hotel Dieu of St. Joseph, Windsor, Ontario

> *Thy shoes shall be iron and brass; and as thy days, so shall thy strength be."—Deuteronomy 33:24-25.*

There was iron and brass in all those heels
when you stepped from the train
toting boxes of medical supplies
and a dream. After meetings and tea
and making your beds in a forsaken
church hall, you traversed the town streets,
a cluster of straight backs and flapping robes,
to find a site for your new hospital
and you did in a large vacant
tract of land—sixteen plots
south of Erie Street. Two months later
you paid for six with all you had
and summoning divine help
to secure the other ten, buried
a statue of St. Joseph head first, topped it
with a boulder and a prayer.
That winter, fed by alms and starved
of hope you could not stop the wind
from penetrating the floor, lifting
the double carpets as you ministered
a few feet from where you slept
to those desperate hands tugging
at your robes, those mouths crying,

Heal me! Save me! at night falling
into the wind's icy arms, lulled to sleep
by the menacing groans of vaulted rafters.

But spring came and you slammed
the door to voices giving bad
advice and squelched those whispers
in your heads telling to you go back
to Quebec.

You knew what you had
to do, and, though the diocese's
coffers were dry and all the bishop
would offer you was freedom
from cloistered commitments, freedom
from a sequestered life, freedom
to venture into the community
to beg at doorsteps
to solicit corporate help
to run a lottery, freedom
to loiter at the horse races, beg
patrons for money
to sew cassocks for priests
to collect and resell stamps
to raise pennies, freedom
to build your hospital
all the while running a day school.

And though you felt an ancient tugging
at your ankles, heard the wind chastising,
Know your place! Fold your hands! Obey!
you didn't stop.

One night, and then another, and another
as you walked the dark road
strewn with moss and fallen trees
relying only on each other and what you knew
you had to do, the moon rose
in the sky and you saw the way
and each morning a chorus of new voices
joined yours and you did it,
the only thing you could do.

Holy Discourse

The Rejection of English speaking applicants for Admission as Postulants to Hotel Dieu Hospital: A Dialogue Between Ontario born Bishop Michael Francis Fallon of Irish descent and Sister Marie de la Ferre, French Canadian.

1. The Bishop's Stand

Thirty Hail Marys in English
would do a lot of good. That
is how you'll draw postulants
to your hospital in great numbers.

Offer clarity, guidance,
nothing less than salvation itself—
but do it in English! Your efforts
will be supported, seen in light,
not the obscurity of a Latin language.

Holy sisters of St. Joseph of Windsor,
fold your praying hands, douse
your vision, bury it deep into
the frozen French province.

We have enough *S'il vous plait*.
Your accent aigus and cedillas
confuse and complicate, voices
evaporate and souls can be damned.

2. Mother Superior's Defense

*Je vous salue, Marie, pleine de grâces,
aidez moi*! A test from heaven,
another challenge
from the bishop's desk:
Why are so many applicants
to your order in Windsor rejected?

Hard to believe, perhaps, but fire
flows through these shrouded veins
of mine and searing words have once
or twice emerged from my pen. Why indeed!
—They were nervous wrecks, I wrote back.
That they did not speak French was—
regrettable, but worse they could
not meet our standards.

Oh, I can sing, reach the high notes
of that other melody, the one voiced
in the name of piety, propriety, but
I'll be damned if I open my hospital
to the shoddy ways of inadequate Anglos
or seal my tongue for the sake
of his most reverend excellency,
Bishop Fallon.

Enough! Today I tended to a withered
man doubled in pain, and later bolstered
a baby who'd emerged from its mother
and both times I thought, this is why

I do it. And I thought, I will not
succumb to ignorance or sloth or
a heavy hand. And I saw myself
standing at the foot of Ouellette
on the shore of the river, felt
the wind under my robes
lifting me over the dark
surface of the water.

Crossing the River

1.

In early afternoon
at the water's edge
I slide into a kayak,
feel a shove from friends.
We will not venture too far,
but follow the shore, turn inland
to the safety of Little River,
duck familiar bridges—
for my sake. Later, spurred
by something, my smile
as I toy with the oar,
or the calm dark surface
of the Detroit River,
or the green lushness
of Peche Island, my guides
point their canoe north
and the river I have only
ever crossed by car over bridge
or through tunnel looms
in front of me, its surface
a thick, wet netherworld.

2.

Between fear and thrill
I tell myself I want to do
this, grip the oar tight, gouge
and drag what I can

of the fluid mass. It's hit
and miss but I adapt
to waves and currents,
my arms spreading
to tentacles of bone
and joint and muscle,
at times my voice
saying, "No, no. This way—
please," my mind squelching
thoughts of lives swallowed here—
a girl I knew who'd jumped,
another who'd driven in, last
summer three boaters caught
in a storm, and accounts
written in history books— the cars
of rumrunners too heavy
for mid-winter ice, the bloody
losses of a pointless war, lives
someone believed were worth living.
My eyes fix on the island, then
on the confident strokes of friends
who've done this a hundred times.

3.

Cities on either side gone,
a canopy of oaks and maples
opens to a haven, uninhabited, water
I can see through. We wend
a reedy maze of canals immersed
in calm, in sounds of warblers,
wood ducks, kingfishers, the plop

of bass or perch breaking
the water's surface. I'm told
there are bald eagles nestled
in these knotted trees.
We exchange pieces of stories:
hauntings of Chippewa casting nets
in these shallow waters once
abundant with aquatic life
and tales of struggles for title,
occupancy, and of curses lain.
On a strip of sandy shore we debark,
stretch, explore the foot path, the bridge
left by whiskey makers with plans.

4.

In late afternoon I am again on open
water. The other side matters now,
the balance of my weight in the craft,
the will of this rolling wet mass
below me, the oar in my hands
working that living chasm of black
that borders the city and lines
my memories, speaks—has always
spoken—saying, this is as far as you
can go, this is where you stop, adjust,
consider the other side. At last I slide
onto the sandy shore, grateful
for its being there, and grateful for
more: the shifting of lines, other
chances, the whims of friends, water
and rock and soil—the outward pull.

Because We Have Lived Here

The streets of Windsor are muraled
memories—dark tones, pastels,
primary colours—all pieces
of experience, tapestries
that hang from doors, walls,
trees, some structures long gone.

I am meeting an old friend
downtown, park the car,
stroll the autumn sun,
my gallery of images.

Here an empty lot soaked
with champagne-coloured tears
for my own awakening,
the skilled hands of a surgeon
saving my breath at thirteen,
tears for the dead, a grandmother
who left me at sixteen to feel
for the first time someone lost
forever and tears for the living,
daughters born, joy I didn't know
was possible,

And here a rich curtain rises
on the bookstore staffed
by a gentle, soft-spoken man
whose eyes seemed to know
the contents of every book he sold,

the bookstore where I bought
my first poems, a selection of classic
and modern verse, photos
and art that opened me
to what words could do.

I am now on the river. To the west
is a hazy form where the Holiday Inn
and Odeon theatre had been, a place
where I dined at the water's edge
with friends and danced to covers
of the Doobie Brothers, gaped
in terror at Spielberg's Jaws.

And closer to where I stand,
my mind traces the form
of a red brick building, a stairway,
the bar where a friend introduced
me to the man I married, a place
whose walls echoed stories
we believed, a place now veiled
in worn pinks and blues.

Before turning south on Ouellette,
I span the Detroit skyline draped
in maroons, purples, charcoals
– awaken images of Hart Plaza,
the downtown humming with people
listening for new sounds and I rouse
grainy front page photographs
of Hudson's imploding, of the glassy

Renaissance Centre being built
to rise above Art Deco skyscrapers
and neogothic spires. I see canvases
of grey smoke surging, buildings afire
with racial tension, a dusty mound
of rubble that had once been
a majestic Detroit City Hall.

At last I arrive, sit in the warm glow
of my favorite restaurant. My friend
whom I have known almost as long
as I have lived here has ordered
my wine, and I relax into the space
where I am, into the person
I have become, meet eyes I know
and that know me as well
as the gauzy reflections
that coat these city streets.

Could It Be The Same City

We've all heard it. *You people are stupid*
pronouncing street names like Pierre,
Peerie. You're losers. (and I'm putting it
nicely). *Really! Who says O-let for Ouellette?*
Who lives in this forgotten Canadian city,
this blue-collar city, "Windsor Ballet" city—
strip-club capital of North America?

I do. And wonder how could it be the same city
whose artists feed my need for Bach, Brubeck or Becket
offering tones, rhythms, words, bolsters; the same city where

a perfect pizza satisfies and a myriad of foods and cultures
nourish, where summers are long, winters mild, and living
affordable. How could it be the same city where

Justice Rand framed labour relations in the spirit of fairness
and compromise, offered a formula later adopted
across Canada, for the sake of working voices; the city whose

river whispers of wars that shaped nations, of slaves
escaped to and from shores, of courage, of victory, loss,
of standing unsure on the edge; the city where

playgrounds sing with joyful cries, where waterways
and marshes sustain my soul and living in the shadow
of what lies to the north forever reminds me of who I am?

Who We Were and What We Could Do
In Honour of Freida Parker Steele

I always heard it said, small steps
make the journey. There's power
in believing in ourselves, of knowing
who we were and what we could do:
work, serve, give back what you can,
my father said. He was the first black
police officer in town when we
weren't let into most bars, weren't allowed
on golf courses, on Boblo Island. Later
he became the first black detective
in Canada. But what's more, Alton Parker
was a good man devoted to fairness.
My mother was as strong, as kind,
as committed to us, as committed
to what was right. Fairer skinned,
she could pass for white and once
signed me up to take piano lessons.
The Ursuline sisters saw my face
and said they had no room for me.
But she knew who I was and made sure
I did too. Years later I did nurses training
at Hotel Dieu, graduated in 1950.
It wasn't easy but again and again,
I came back to what I'd learned,
to what we'd learned.

We learned to navigate hate. Timing
mattered, little things mattered.
My parents had forged for me
a skin of iron that I could slip into
if I needed to protect myself
and I needed it a lot back then.

One night at the Edgewater,
celebrating with some forty other
graduating nurses, the glamorous
and famous bar owner Bertha Thomas
whom Maclean's magazine had called
"beautiful . . . full of personality"
took me and another black nurse
by our arms, lead us to the door
of her club, leaned into us saying,
*don't make a scene. I will not have
my other guests offended.* It hurt.
A piece of me was on fire, but I grounded
each step in the knowledge that I would
work here, I would let my fairer friends revel
without incident that night, and iron-clad,
I let the firm grip of Bertha Thomas
lead me out the door.

Next day, word spread. The mayor's
daughter who was with us that night
told her dad what Bertha had done.
He was furious and made sure
people knew it. Days later the Star's
columnist, R. M. Harrison, pounded

out a scathing piece in my defence
and though not mentioned by name,
the famous bar keeper was in the news
again. What mattered more,
we were in the news again
and people talked again
about what was right,
what was wrong.

There was a lot of hate back then,
still is today, but I made my way
around it and through it, sure
in that iron skin of mine,
in who I was, what I could do,
in the small steps I could take.

My Father Outside the Chrysler Assembly Plant, 1955

You are twenty-five, standing
outside the Chrysler assembly plant
at two in the afternoon, in line since
five a.m.—waiting your turn.
For the third time in two days
you've reached the front
of the line, twice been told
by the watchman to move
to the back as others with paler
complexions were admitted,
interviewed, signed up
for real work, real pay.

It is 1955. You've washed dishes,
chopped vegetables sixteen hours
a day at the Sunnyside Tavern, need
a better job, will stand here, stand
this. Now, next in line before
that same watchman, you believe
this time must be different, this time
he will not turn you away.

Habit lowers your eyes. You know
he is eyeing the man behind you,
Hey Jack! You're up! You (his finger
now in your face) *go back to the end
of the line.* There is derision in his voice.
Something snaps. Your eyes meet his,

your hand seizes his collar. *You sonofa…,*
stop mid-sentence, face wrenched
with rage. He sneers pushes back,
Get your filthy wop hands off me,
he scowls. You sock him in the nose.
In a second he is on his back,
an officious secretary barks
into a phone from a temporary office
set up just outside the plant door.
What the hell's going on here?
It's another man. With hands,
and arms and heavy accent
you plead understanding.
He laughs, rolls his eyes, shakes
his head. Pow! Your fist explodes
again. Your mouth spews
accusations in a foreign tongue.
In a flash, you come back, feel
regret. Not again, not again.

It is no wonder you don't expect
the police officer's kind eyes, his attempt
to understand your words, a wife
in hospital, a new baby, debts owed.
Your passion, regret, sheepish eyes,
rounded shoulders win him over.
You tell him you'd kiss the hands
of those you've hit to get work.
He knows you mean it, negotiates,
mediates, works magic, charges
are stayed. You even get the job.

Today, you laugh as you recall
how those men you cuffed
became your friends, how they'd pat
your back when you passed them
in the plant, how you knew
not to look into their eyes
for too long.

In a Downtown Windsor Restaurant
for Ray Manzarol

Friday night at Mario's, dimly lit,
downtown street lights splashing
the window panes, the air redolent
with oregano, basil, rosemary, garlic,
parmesan, you offer your saxophone
to novice and seasoned listeners
despite the clinking of cutlery and glass,
above the muffled din of voices.
The notes are clean, each musical phrase
a wave of melancholy, joyfulness,
or soulfulness. We are tuned
to the lift and weight

of your hands on the instrument, your lips
on the mouthpiece.

Your sound threads us to each other, grounds us
to this place, cradles us in this moment
and I sweep the faces of men and women
and children in the room, wonder
about our collective losses, our gains
what we will never know about each other,
your tone
        holding the gravity of it all,
the control of your breath
        holding the counter weight
that lifts,
lifts,
keeping it together,
keeping us all together.

Peter Hrastovec

Born and raised in Windsor, Ontario, **Peter Hrastovec** and his wife Denise have three wonderful children. They have recently experienced the joy of grandparenthood. Peter's first book of poetry, *In Lieu of Flowers* is in its third printing. His most recent book of poetry, *Sidelines*, was edited by the student interns of the Editing and Publishing Practicum at the University of Windsor. When he is not writing, practising law or pursuing community projects, Peter is happy to perform in community theatre.

Walkerville Reflections

I live and breathe this city. It has a "take it or leave it" vibe, its own rhythm—a lunch bucket snap, a car door thump, a siren's squeal. Here labor and management break bread, volunteers abound, a shared idea takes wing and road hockey is king. It is a city where I can forgive and where I am forgiven.

Windsor is my life and historic Walkerville my home.

The easy part was to say "yes" to the innovative Marty G. and to embrace this project, a journey with several gifted writers. The hard part was to capture what had been lost or forgotten in this town and try, as much as we dared, to resurrect the past. This team pioneered on—without compass, map or intellectual GPS. We yacked, clawed at each other's drafts and drew inspiration from our collective task.

As a young man, I didn't appreciate the rich local history—the root fabric of characters and incidents woven into a celebrated folkloric tapestry. As I grew older, raised a family, worked and played, rested and wrote, I had come to realize that this unique little city on the south shore of a fabled river was its own social experiment. And this enclave where I have lived most of my adult life—Olde Walkerville—boasts as many ghosts as it does current residents. Whisky barons, labourers, the wealthy and the average folk shared the common denominator of a story in need of telling.

Together, we writers discovered a shared thread—everything has its own story. The romance of world history gives way to looking no further than outside one's own front door. The desire to preserve a memory of a place or a person puts a choke hold on your psyche and doesn't let go until you get it right.

I stepped from cobblestone onto asphalt, from cracked staircases into modern elevators, walked shadowed footsteps and hopefully left an imprint or two of my own on this all-too-familiar terrain, this storied landscape that vaunts such indefinable charm. In the end, we accept history, regardless of the recurring pain or the measured losses. I only hope that those we remember and honour here find a way to forgive us.

Heppenstall's

there was this sign
across the river
there on the north bank
beaming ardent red
ruddy and real
its letters
scorching shadows
inviting the night

there was this sign
that marked the place
across the river
here on its south bank
where we were
where we weren't
supposed to be
a sign that triggered
warnings admonitions
and demands
for avoidance
for abstinence
for averting
this legendary location
a mile across water
where mysteries
were revealed
and passion
collided head-on
with clumsiness

there was a sign
you looked for
that didn't glow
in the dark
or rest on the banks
of any river
a sign found
in her eyes
a deliberate sign
that said
"it" was alright

Land-Castered

they parked you at the river
decommissioned by default
a victim of age and obsolescence
where for fifty cents of
a mother's hard-earned money
a wonder-struck boy could
climb into your dormant shell
ask innumerable questions
about bomb bays and ballistics
and stand slack jawed in the shadow
cast by your mammoth wings

they raised you on a pedestal
like one of those plastic toy models
high above the rose bed
high above the names of the dead
boys turned men   soldiers turned heroes
who'd argue that you were their life's adventure
for the havoc you caused   the hunger you fed
the lives you saved   the freedom you restored
yours was the confluence of misery and salvation
and the reward earned for the victory you enabled
this right to remain silent in solitude

now grounded in a hangar
lifeless for lack of parts
the idealists scatter the globe
to piece together your resurrection
urged by visions of roaring rolls royce engines

and the gleam of your shimmering fuselage
slicing the low-lying clouds
what they would give, these dreamers and the dead,
to see your frail beauty lumbering along ancient flight paths
with the deafening reassurance that once again
your legend has taken wing

Number One Navajo

as a rule
you can build
a house on a road
named for an aboriginal people
so long as the road and the land
do not belong to the people

there is a difference

you would think that a house
bearing the address
number one navajo
rested on aboriginal lands
for the road named after
a native people who have resided
for centuries on sacred lands
in arizona, utah, new mexico
thousands of miles away
had no connection
to the enclave created
by the father of fire water

distance makes a difference

when mr. a. w. reid,
businessman,
commissioned
mr. d. j. cameron,
architect,

to design and build
his new art deco home in 1924
on a plot of land
with municipal address
number one navajo
it didn't occur to either of them
that reid, his neighbours
or the folks on cayuga
just one street over
would be the pillars
of political incorrectness
some sixty years later
long after reid, cameron
(and the neighbours) were dead

then a different thought

through municipal machination
cayuga and navajo are joined
by the umbilical cord of urbanization
that gave birth to willistead crescent
as unaboriginal a name as ever there was

some differences take their time
some differences remain long after landowners,
their builders and their neighbours die
covenants in deeds and instruments of title
language sacrosanct with a smattering of latin
convey the notion that it was good to
restrict new neighbours on account
of religion and color and ethnicity

puritanical thinking that inspired the
quick closing of doors
the denial of entry
a roadblock to tolerance

in time things become different

change welcomed   language dismantled
foundations of law made equals of all
the houses remained the stories chronicled
new families with new names arrive and thrive
in once forbidden neighbourhoods
in houses on streets once-named
for proud aboriginal peoples
in these houses
in these homes
new generations flourish
and embrace the difference

A Stable Influence

every autumn of every year
in the same spot in front
of the nun's hospital
a scene from the nativity
appeared without fanfare
stable cows shepherds
first-time parents
and a newborn
poof—like magic

every year a wise old man
dictated where and how
to place the statues
this was not a random act
it required thought
and a tactical plan
precise amounts of straw
magi angled deliberately
proximity of cows to manger
all measured exactly
for everyone knew
it was the animals' breath
that provided warmth
to this make shift lodging
in frosty old bethlehem

with strategic solemnity
this story was always told
the message delivered

every year without fail
until the old man left
and the nuns disappeared
and the hospital converted
to all things secular
the statuary buried
in crates in storage

there is an art to everything
and in every art a reason
and somewhere a newborn
forever swaddled
waits for his return

TOOLS
—inspired by a photo at Colonial Tool dated November 1950

the climb to the top
was always a challenge

in this old relic of a building
the laborious ascent is breathtaking
steep stairs defy current building codes
as pumping hearts channel high and away
from the dull thud
the pernicious pounding
of the ever-droning factory below

the climb to the top
is always a challenge

before facing oak and mahogany
hewn leather and ancient cigar smells
the money and the might
stumble upon a plain wood frame
dozens of black and white smiles
men in factory jackets and work clothes
assembled like athletes in rows
grinning with gratitude like maniacs
under the direction
of some forgotten shutterbug

the climb to the top
has challenges
they are now old

they are now dead
they are old and dead
leaving widows sons daughters
wealth debt and legends
and the team-like precision
of their wide-eyed leers

the climb to the top
can challenge

there is always one
who looks away from the camera
the one guy in every group
who draws attention to himself
his eyes captivated by a pretty girl
or wandering in wont of a passing car
or caught in a day dream in progress
the one guy who begs questions

the climb to the top
is often lonely

they were asked to sit
not in protest nor at rest
not a union break or lunch
someone must have thought
it would be a good idea
to capture the moment
this collective history
the photograph doesn't lie
it tells stories

it says nothing
it exists so that
someone would someday
climb to the top of these stairs
and stare back

a slow descent
can be uneventful

nothing changes
not the stairs
the building nor the factory
only the movement
the methodical stepping
the careful decline
to the bottom
with ghosts who
smirk from above
in the wake
of blind ambition

Movements

In memory of Stephen Marshall

politics is power
fueled by dollars   politics becomes
the art of accomplishing   anything

the old town hall   in walkerville
built in 1904   in a new century   for fifteen thousand dollars
on the existing foundation of a demolished church
less expensive   they said
to build a shrine to authority
where once stood a house of god
the irony eludes the city fathers and the whisky kings
the sarcasm starched out of their souls

abandoned by amalgamation   the politics of unification
the town disappears into the past
the old town hall is no longer the old town hall
it morphs into diverse uses
becomes just another building
destined for the wrecking ball

comes along a new generation
movers and shakers
determined to preserve to protect
to ensure khan's clever design
of quoins and burst pediment
is not reduced to dust
they raise more than in 1904
to move revive and   restore

to turn the corner
and place this
red brick monolith
at a new address
with new life
at the end of the block
on an old street
at the end of the century

the old town hall
once built in the wrong place   to save money
the old town hall
moved to the right place   saves us

Emily Carr Hangs in a Gallery
— *Yan Mortuary Poles, 1928/1929*

when i first saw her
child-eyed and gullible
emily carr hung
in a stairwell
in a gallery that
once was a mansion
built by whisky
in a town turned city

she moved with the gallery
to a building
that once was a brewery
that wasn't built by whisky
and was widely popular
(the brewery—not the gallery)
in a city that remained a city

with a roll of the dice
comes a casino and
poor emily is shipped
across town
to a shopping mall
in the middle of the city

where she becomes hugely popular
(not so much as the brewery)
and shoppers turned art buffs
mill about with bundles and bags
talk post-impressionism and
a thirty percent discount on shoes

the gallery hits the jackpot
moves upstream to sacred land
(remember the brewery turned casino?)
vacant and demolished
and a glass and steel totem
rises from the hallowed earth
to house the art
where emily endures

i see her again
with aging eyes
revived

Anti-Theatre

if all the world's a stage
this space missed the cut
a once proud proscenium
home to orchestras ethnic
dancers and battling bands
now houses fertilizer potted
plants and drainage tile
coiled like slumbering snakes

this concrete shell tucked
in the middle of a park
in the middle of the day
would erupt in sonorous
sounds of angelic voices
or the rhythmic tapping
of tender well-trained feet
outdoor amphitheatre
once proud centre piece
for art and performance
now a go-to-hub for tools
trucks trailers and tractors
chipped and cracked
wrecked and worn-out
your bricks and mortar
could tell a story or two
or resonate with tuneful
tasteful echoes

if only the crew at parks and rec
would lay down their tools
slip off their boots
circle up join hands
and dance the dance
of their forefathers
the dance that defined
a generation or two
in sync and in harmony

Open Sore
—in memoriam, G.M. Transmission Plant, Windsor, Ontario

at the edge of the town
your once-upon-a-time farm thrived
corn and wheat flourished
and cattle foraged in languid splendor
under an unhurried sun

your farm gave way
to stockyards
teeming with promise
and a wily old distiller
who pumped his aromatic mash
into his fattening cattle
decreeing that there
would be no waste
amassing his herds
and his fortune
in the daily rush to market

your stockyards gave way
to your shiny new factory
fabricated steel and bulging concrete
oozing grease oil and potential
where sturdy men sweat
and yielded new harvests
of engines axles and chassis

when the gods of necessity asked
you answered with guns and munitions

and followed the frenzy
with reparations repairs and refurbishment

and then came transmissions—
tons and tons of gear boxes
for wheels cars and trucks
torqueing and spinning
engineered and engine assembled
trained in and built-out
expanding and growing
on your sixty acres
like a post-industrial fungus

you welcomed thousands
men and women
who worked who toiled
who fought for wages
earned their keep
fed their families
clothed their children
and gave them education
profits were made
retirements planned
and the future
never in question
while the metal machine chorus
continued to sing

and then silence
your factory closed
and we paused

holding our collective breath
like an audience waiting for the
magician's next trick and then
—nothing

the show was over
your factory gave way
to a demolition crew
and an assurance
that reclamation led to profits
that copper brass aluminum
plastic glass and steel
moved at market price

and so began the great dismantling
the ripping and rending
slashing and shredding
grinding and crushing
accumulations bundles piles
burial mounds in your sacred space

yours the large gaping hole
that festers in the middle of the city
ours the wide irreparable
tear in the muscled heart
raw unyielding
bruised and unbending
exhausted under the weight
of this daily condemnation
that ruins the land
with rivers of blood-red rust

the hurt as heavy as metal
your people are numbed
by your attrition
their oral history muted
by teeth clenched
in unrelenting rage

this very earth
scorched and sullied
wrecked and wretched
is an unholy deprivation
of opportunity soured
it gives off an acrid odour
like the century's old mash
that once filled the nostrils
of the unsuspecting livestock
who knew little of milk and
nothing of slaughter and for whom
the invention of transmissions
or instruments of war
were not foretold

and the plight of
the laid-off auto worker
never a concern
to unwary heifers
grazing in fields
their only job
to live off the fat
of the land

Shaughnessy's Gone To Pelee

she would command
attention with
her big dogs tethered
big smile beaming
big laughter roaring
riotously deafening
a commanding woman
onboard the little boat
bound for the big island

at the law firm
the lawyers would explain
"Shaughnessy's gone to Pelee"
her office—the island

self-proclaimed island queen
without pedigree
palace or postage stamp
a carriage turned pickup truck
destined for an inland farm
her broke-down fiefdom
hospitable and homey
she poured beer better
than a bar maid
and told stories
that filled the room
like a larder at harvest
a dyed-in-the-wool-politico
she'd cut to the chase
the acute cross-examiner

at the courthouse
the staff would say
"Shaughnessy's gone to Pelee"
her court—her stage

she could charm a grizzly bear
arm wrestle a communist
dance on a bed of flowers
and humour those who despair
with a good joke
clean or dirty
restaurants knew her
shopkeepers wooed her
police would clear the way
for her personal parade

how is it then
with so much
more to do
with so much
more to accomplish
when finally she
became the island
from where
she could shout
she is silenced
our queen is dead
her final words
etched in stone
hushed among weeds
and wild rhubarb

after the wake
the mourners would say
"Shaughnessy's gone to Pelee"
home—to rest

and man
this island
her island
has never
been the same
since her return
to the earth

Dorothy Mahoney

Born in Windsor, **Dorothy Mahoney** has several books of poetry. Most recent is *Off-Leash* (Palimpsest Press, 2016) with another to be published in 2020.

Ford City

I listen. I have always been a listener. I listen and look for certain details like: the bronze bird in Mark Williams' sculpture, the priest's heart floating in a glass jar in Michael Power's book (1986), and the car tires at the Border City Boxing Club.

I write these into a compressed context. The 17th century Japanese poet, Basho, wrote travel anecdotes along with haiku which became known as *haibun*. I like to play with this form, compressing the prose and jumping to a haiku. The title, prose and haiku become a triangle, linked to each other, yet separate. I edit and edit until it is in its simplest form.

Although I did not grow up in Ford City, I am happy to see the continuous revival, having attended the Open Street celebration there last summer. Things are happening. A microbrewery plans to establish itself there, and unique businesses are taking hold.

A new history builds.

Searching for Jesus

He stood at the top of the stairs
his arms out
in a hug you know would bring you close
to his open heart. I still look, passing or stopped,
at the light
of Riverside Drive and Drouillard,

How long he waited there,
in squalls off the Detroit River,
his welcoming arms, ready.
A hundred years when rioting parishioners
refused to let the new priest inside.
Women with broomsticks, police with billy clubs.
The bishop's threats to close it down.
The heart of the old priest floating
in a glass jar in the sacristy.

Now the Lady of the Rosary Church
sells for a dollar:
the altar a stage for wedding bands,
the confessional a cloakroom,
the pews refurnished into a bar,
Jesus gone missing.

Some distance down the road
the Romanian Orthodox church
full of incense and once a month
the sale of fried
onions and pierogis.

Father Simion chuckles,
"Of course,
so that's where he came from."

Jesus at the entrance
of the Lady of the Rosary Cemetery.

Sand

Words like sand
filtering funneling foundry sand
brought by barge, mountains of sand
and the heat and the fire,
casting, and the feral cat that someone fed
and so many doors closed but at shift change
doors open and drinks wait at watering holes that only
regulars know and they know you and you know
how illegal weapons melt down to what is cast
and the leftover sand is used as fill for foundations of houses
now deemed old and many torn down, many gone
who lived here and left when the foundry closed but
those who stayed and hung on with words you might say
could turn to curse, could stave the cold, could be
sand that fills the cracks that makes
the mold that moves the world with furtive words that turn like
wheels
in sand

Border City Boxing

In a border city, boxers here go over there,
and they come here from places where they sweat,
train to be their best like Kronks or Detroit gyms where
famous people drop in to raise some funds and someone
says Madonna and Rachel Ray but here the picture on
the wall is Justin before Prime Minister when he
was starting out and came by, dropped his clothes to work
out and Jackknife Josh got in a straight right.
Well this here is the Border City Boxing Club and this is
where the legends start: Sweet Sammy, Andre Gorgeous,
Jeannine Garside, and Margaret Sidoroff three-time world champion bigger

than life- size on a mural outside.

This is Border City in Ford City,
this is where the gloves go on, the sparring starts,
the kick it up a notch. Say Joe Louis, Sugar Ray, Rocky Marciano.
You've got to feel it, work it, want it, you're 100 % in or you're out.
You can't 'play' boxing like basketball or baseball. You're all in.
This is Border City, where half a tire anchored to a wall is for
upper cuts and jabs, the tire in the metal frame is for sledge hammer
and the two tires heaped on the floor, you raise them, raise them high.
This is Ford City. One. Two. One. Two.

Down the Road

His mother took him to see the Queen when she came down Drouillard. He was too young to remember. 'Dressed in his shirt and shorts. Immigrants. His father worked construction, rode a bicycle, built a house on Albert. A concrete block basement with a cement floor, shelved with wine. He rearranged the bottles. His father doesn't know he sold it to friends who left with duffel bags full. Later, trouble: gangs, motorcycles, the Lobos' clubhouse and the Queensmen. It was a tough neighbourhood but when the ten-year-old girl was killed on Hickory, his mother said it was time to go.

green tomatoes
on the windowsill,
she turns them

The Memory of Water

When the American cousin gave his mother's eulogy, he made her young again, swimming to Peche Island and back with the cottager who would become his dad, watching her rise from the water, so sure, so right. It was a different river then. People swam in it, before it was dredged deeper as a shipping canal, before swift currents, before Jacques Cousteau proclaimed the Great Lakes in trouble. Down river, in old photographs hand-tinted blue, girls with bare legs at the municipal bathing beach near Ford City. No swimming now. Until this night along Riverside Drive, we stop. A lone deer before us, swam across from Belle Isle. Sleek. Steady. And we wonder if it can fight the current, swim back.

arms sore
throwing stones into the river
farther

Passing time

My whole attitude changed that summer, Bill tells me as he
chops an apple. He's making oatmeal on the stove, dismisses instant.
He worked at Filwood Industries. They made bodies for garbage
trucks and later military vehicles during the war. (I never heard of it.)
It's the Caboto Club parking lot now, he says. It was noisy, dirty.
The door panels heavy. They hung from rings to move them along.
At the end, these had to be cut, knocked off and the panels smoothed
with a grinder. Instead, he spends a day grinding and grinding each
ring down. It doesn't matter what you do, if you look good doing it,
he laughs as he reaches for cinnamon.

shift change
wiping the counter
clock-wise

Generations

It's about conversations. Mark Williams is convinced. Painting murals outside, right on the walls, people stop and talk, pull out their wallets, show birth certificates. Birthplace: Ford City. Point to where the Ford plant used to be and Ford City Hall; cars jammed all up and down the place. Thousands of workers. More than three million vehicles made. Bronze men weld their details along a car roof in his sculpture: Jacques, McGuire, Gaudette. Standing as their fathers stood. Sweat bronzed on foreheads. Speaking with their eyes.

sparrows gather, disperse
a bronze bird
stays

Mary Ann Mulhern

Black Moss Press has published six books of poetry by **Mary Ann Mulhern**. Her first book, *The Red Dress*, received national attention on the CBC radio program, Tapestry. *Touch the Dead* and *When Angels Weep* were short-listed for the Acorn-Plantos Award. Her newest book, *How We Fare* is inspired by events in the news. *Selected Poems* by Mary Ann Mulhern will be published by Black Moss Press, April 2018.

Riverside

When I moved to Riverside in Windsor in the nineties, I had no realization of the history, the vitality of human existence, over the previous century. Thus, when asked to research events, and write poetry, I was curious and intrigued by the stories I read and heard. In the instance of Peche Island, which is located directly across the river from my residence, the legend of "a curse" amazed me. How could this seemingly peaceful, lovely island harbour something so dark, so haunting and, by all accounts, alive to this day? In my poem, "Curse of Peche Island", I use narrative poetry to "tell the story". Rosalie Laforet was a widow who survived on four acres of Peche Island by hunting, fishing and farming. Her family had lived there for over a hundred years, and had formed ties with the Ojibway, who taught the Laforets how to prepare and store food for winter. In 1928, Hiram Walker, a very wealthy man, demanded the entire island so that he could establish a haven for the rich. Rosalie defended her right to remain. Walker and his lawyer sent thugs to destroy her winter food, thereby forcing her to leave. She dropped to her knees and proclaimed a curse, "I curse this island, you and your families. Nothing will ever thrive here, ever prosper." I have no doubt that Walker and his henchman laughed and dismissed her curse as the folly of a superstitious old woman!

Walker oversaw the design and building of a forty-room mansion, golf course, peach orchards, docks for yachts and river-boats. In less than two years, lightning hit the mansion in the night. Explosive flames could be seen throughout Riverside. Only concrete foundations remain to this day. The poems I've written, especially, "Curse of Peche Island", "tell the story" of Rosalie Laforet's curse, and how it continues to resound a century later- nothing has ever been successfully developed on Peche!

Glengarda School for children with learning and developmental issues was founded by the Sisters of St. Ursala in 1939. At that time, no other school accepted these students. The original building served as school and convent. Glengarda closed and was torn down in the nineties. Prior to demolition, I drove there several times to sketch the entrance. Today, luxury condos rule the property.

As a former nun and retired special-education teacher, I took great interest in writing about Glengarda. A poem that resonates strongly with me is: "Bones of Glengarda" Days before demolition, permission was given for anyone to remove articfacts, door handles, name-plates of nuns, etc. I confess that I prize an ornate door-handle, and a name-plate. At the same time, I recognize this as "a trespass".

I've always been intrigued by Bertha Thomas, who owned and managed "Thomas Inn" in prohibition times. Bertha possessed the wit and savvy to evade police and inspectors. She served liquor and entertained gambling without any significant interference. Bertha squelched neighbourhood negativity by being extremely generous. She paid for hair-cuts for boys, provided for needy children, and always sent "baskets of candy" at Christmas. I enjoyed writing "Inn of Prohibition" and "Blessing of Riverside". From my balcony I can see an abandoned red-brick factory, one wall clearly lettered:

"Riverside Brewery Co. The Taste Tells" There was an ad showing two fathers with young children, all drinking beer. That ad today would be unthinkable!

Just last year, Abars, the last roadhouse from prohibition times, was torn down. I watched the demolition, and imagined the events that may have occurred in those historic rooms. Legend speaks of Al Capone, motor-cycle gangs, loud and fierce. In more recent years, many neighbourhood people enjoyed the deck on the water, along with good food, beer and wine. To me, the "ghost of Abars" will always linger over that generous and grassy piece of land by the Detroit River.

Finally, I've written "Brides of MacKenzie Hall". When I visited MacKenzie Hall last summer, I realized they now hold weddings there. In the poem, I wonder how many brides know anything of the history of the stately building,- courtroom, prison, gallows, cemetery. I also wonder how many couples stand beneath the iron gibbit and read inscriptions of those unfortunates whose hanged bodies were displayed. We'll never know if there were innocent men who suffered this fate.

Writing these "Riverside Poems" has given me a very different perspective on the landscape in which I live here in the city of Windsor, ON.

Curse of Peche Island

My curse settles over Peche Island
Mist of breath, dark net of words
I, Rosalie Laforet, curse you, your families, this island
Nothing will ever prosper, ever thrive

A woman alone on this land
My four acres nurture me
Through seasons of snow, wind, rain and sun
My table laden with grapes, apples, peaches, rabbit, pickerel and perch
Taken into fists, a wealthy man, his lawyer
Grey suits woven with greed

They build a mansion, forty rooms
Persian rugs, mirrors from France
A banquet hall, staircase carved from oak
Until shafts of fire
Steal into every space
Rage across the sky
Ashes fly into heated winds
Settle over foundations left to rot

Who recalls a widow on swollen knees
Hears echoes of her prophecy
Only owls, deer, foxes, swans and geese
Racer snakes coiled on rocks
Eagles with bloodied talons , torture of prey
The specter of a summer mansion
Embraced by shadows
Eternal words of a woman's curse
Midnight music of the moon

Ruins of a Mansion

I stand over mossy ruins
Hiram Walker's mansion of forty rooms
I long to walk those fabled halls
Dance in salons papered red
Dine at the table set with porcelain
Waterford crystal filled with wine
White roses freshly cut

The island mocks me
A wilderness, trees, rocks and vines
Rosalie Laforet's legacy prevails
I feel her spirit, hear her voice
Whispers of a curse

Peaches from the River

Elizabeth Walker enters rooms
Of her father's mansion
Feels the silence of space
Something hidden in corners
Impression of words, smothered
Drowned in darkened shoals

Elizabeth tends the peach orchard
Climbs a ladder, thins full branches
Waits for the August harvest
Golden, round, juicy and sweet

She commands every basket
Cast into a hungry river
Peaches bob over waves
Pile into nets of boaters
An easy catch, enough for pastry and pie
Amber jars on a winter shelf

To Keep a Distance

The sun keeps an eye on Peche
So does the red-rimmed moon
Stars keep their distance
The island bears a curse
Echoes of words from a widow's lips
"I curse you, I curse this island
Nothing will ever flourish here"

Peche knows her rightful owner
Keeps watch for wealthy thieves
Disguise of suits, dark and grey
Legal papers blackened with ink
Poison

Child of Glengarda

I am a child of Glengarda
The only school open to me
A boy with pathways to Math, Science, Reading
Blocked from birth
Sisters of St. Ursala take me by the hand
Offer paint, pencils, paper and chalk
All the colours of earth, rainbows of sky

Stars reveal stories, pictures and words
The Big Dipper, Orion, Cassiopeia
Whole worlds shine upon me

Every night I look up
Revelations of the universe
A nun with a cross on her breast
Pointing to the heavens
Leading me there.

Bones of Glengarda

We have permission to trespass
Before machines bite into bones of Glengarda
Crowds swarm the halls, sacred space of a convent
A holy cloister, forbidden.

We remove cast-iron handles, heavy, ornate
Names of nuns under small metal plates
Sister Marie Clare, Sister John Thomas, Sister St. Rose, Sister Theresa
Virgins who slept, prayed, and studied here.

We have permission
To take pieces of lives
Never meant to be touched
We have permission to trespass.

Playboy at Glengarda

A teen-aged boy shares pages of paradise
Blondes, brunettes, redheads, full glory of flesh
Mother St. Pius prays for divine guidance
The Phys Ed teacher offers redemption
Curiosity—normal for any boy

The teen embraces every temptress
Dreams of bare bosoms, bikini bottoms
Long shiny hair, lips kissed with crimson sin,
Open

The magazine is shredded, burned
It displays Satan's smile.

To Keep Vigil

Ten thousand cars pass by

Nuns cast in black, keep vigil
Over the relic of Glengarda
Sentinels who watch over memory
Mysteries of Literature, Math, Music, Science
Endless wonder of young minds
A school gone silent in the shadow of a high-rise
Vanish of rain and fog
White mantel of snow

Ten thousand cars pass by

St. Ursala's Sculptor

A young sculptor named Christopher
Shapes St. Ursala leading a child
Across a bridge of light
He uses ancient tools, chisel and caliper
Thumb and forefinger, imprints of art

She graces the foyer of a high-rise
Ghost of Glengarda
Christopher Rees folds his hands in death
Blessings of St. Ursala
Warm his winter grave
Snow brushes over stone
Words and numbers vanish
Like a young man's breath
Stolen in whims of a sudden storm

Abars

The last roadhouse from prohibition days
Shivers in Windsor winds
Voices of rum-runners echo in halls
Smoke from Capone's cigar drifts
Across decades, legends and lies

Rooms and tables empty now
Motor-cycle tales left behind
Machines fill parking lots
Jaws ready to devour what remains

Earth prepares a generous grave
Layers of soil, gravel, sand and clay

In golden hours of sunset
Abars raises a glass to us
As we pass along river and road
Here's to friendship, long life
The good times!

An Inn of Prohibition

Thomas Inn on the river—
In the polished dining room
Scotch, bourbon, brandy, bath-tub gin
Champagne at tables, poker, blackjack, baccarat

Bertha Thomas wore fur, silk, strands of pearls,
Met ten policemen at the door
Her hands stacked with money,
Lovely Bertha sauntered to the far exit,
Twenty-dollar bills dropping
Before hungry men with badges
All of them on their knees,
Bertha, their queen
And they her faithful servants

Blessing of Riverside

Bertha Thomas knew the wrath of neighbourhood tales
How they shaped into shadows across windows and doors
Spawned suspicion of Bertha, her inn.

She sent bright posters to every house
Offers of free hair-cuts for boys
Coats to warm kids at the bus-stop
Mittens—red, purple, blue, green and white
Balls of wool knitted into favours of welcome
Christmas baskets, books, candy, toys
Protection from shards of glass, black paint on walls
Scribbles of hate on sidewalks, reports to police

Bertha Thomas,
The blessing of Riverside!

The Taste Tells

1926, Riverside Brewery Co. opened—
Vats of beer poured into thirsty mouths
Every bottle bragged, "the taste tells".

There was an ad. two fathers, small children,
Guzzling beer in the Windsor sun
As if beer replaced milk, nourished little ones
Built strong bones and teeth, refreshing!

After ninety years the photo shocks,
Shouts of abuse, babes led astray
Now kids sneak a sip of Dad's latest brew

And the taste tells.

Brides of MacKenzie Hall

MacKenzie Hall in Sandwich Town
Hosts weddings in spring, summer, winter, fall
Satin-covered chairs, champagne kisses
Dancing past the mid-night hour

How many white-veiled brides know the stories
Chiseled into grey-stone walls
Court-house, prison, gallows, graves

How many lovers hold hands
Beneath the iron gibbet
Feel the cold breath of ghosts
Mingle of misery
An escaped slave returned to shackles
Two men who crossed the river
To murder the owner of a café
Both hanged in jeers of a rainy dawn
Broken bodies displayed
Between bars of the gibbet
Curious crowds stood in line
As if before a coffin with a cross
Maybe a few whispered prayers
While others savored hell.

What bride and groom
Take heed of the parking lot
Unclaimed corpses, scattered skeletons
Buried beneath the pave of black.

Vanessa Shields

Vanessa Shields' passion for literary arts begins in her heart and extends onto pages, into classrooms and onto stages. Though she lives and works in Windsor with her family, she loves to travel for readings and teaching. Her first book, *Laughing Through A Second Pregnancy* is a comedic memoir, and her two books of poetry, *I Am That Woman* and *Look At Her* express her life's duality as a mother and a writer in an honest, brave, sensual way. Windsor holds the key to her writing heart.

Reflections on Being a Poet in the City of Windsor

When I was nineteen, I bought a one-way ticket from my hometown Windsor, Ontario to Kelowna, British Columbia. My innocent and inexperienced heart urged me to leave and explore, to experience living in a new place with strangers, to step into unfamiliar landscapes, and to embark upon adventures that seemed otherwise unavailable to the yearnings of my soul. Yet, within six months I would return to the city of my birth, my home—as the place to heal my body, as the place where love began. And friendship and family too. A place to feel the almost intangible sense of purpose that resonates in the solar plexus when you come to accept that this is the place where you belong.

Though I've often travelled abroad seeking adventure and inspiration, I've always returned to this city of fractured identity. I know the bumps in her roads, her empty spaces (old and new), and her aromas rising from my favourite restaurants and homes. I've huddled in her darkest corners where our secrets shiver together. And I've written poems inspired by theses muses, and what I have uncovered in my own past and present experience of Windsor.

It is true one *chooses* her city—as I have chosen Windsor as the one I call home, despite having felt at *home* in many other incredible places. The stories I tell or re-tell in my poetry come to me in powerful bursts of pride, frustration, humility, curiosity and emotion. I write to piece together the fractures in my own sense of belonging and identity, and like this city, the more I delve deep into it, the more I have faith in the beauty that this wild state-of-being upholds.

Double-Sessions At Wheels Roller Rink
Circa 1988, Dougall Avenue

Dreams invoked on Saturday afternoons
Doing double-sessions at Wheels Roller Rink

This ten-year-old girl with burgeoning anorexia
Found order at the rental skate counter

Cubbies holding eight-wheeled freedom machines
Brown-beige community skates a slight embarrassment

Forgiven by sipping blue Slush Puppies and chomping
Skinny string red licorice while scoping out the regulars

Couldn't take my eyes off the dulled black tight-jeaned butts
Bright white or striped hair picks poking out of pockets

How smooth his long brown mullet
How plump her halo black afro

I wanted to be those teenagers swapping spit and gum
Near the lockers tongues so quick I didn't blink as I stared

Eyes of tigers made me not stop believing that I could
Make the couples slow-dance skate

Lights switched from bold to bendy
To match the beat of young love

Round and round pushing over smooth gray painted floor
Gentle leg lift sit on one boot kick out other watch my skills

I could do it too Punchinello from the zoo
Backwards swerved weaved through pairs

My palms open waiting for that special boy
To choose me spin me out of my oblivion

I Want to Know What Love is
Lanspeary Park Ice Rink circa 1985, Ottawa Street and Langlois

On the Lanspeary park ice
Foreigner blared from watchful speakers
Serenading my impure thoughts for
The teenage ref skating with such gorgeous precision

I wanted to know what love is
Love icy unsmooth
Slippery when wet
Scratched and bladed

My wobbly knees knocking on his country's frozen land
My tender ankles shaking in desperation
I would show him what love is

Off I whooshed to catch the white snow of his sideways stop
Pushing and gliding my mission with 7-year-old faith
I stunted a fall to get his attention
Arms and legs splayed spinning on my stomach
Bumped dirty wood boards with a thud to match the beat
Of 80s love-song unbridled begging
My plan would impress even the zamboni driver

Blue-knitted mitten to my chin to hold fake pain
Michelle my friend yelled speed-skated to me
Crashed into the boards sliding down
My plan-breaking parallel and out   kicked   her leg and
Into my lower lip her toe pick pierced

I wanna feel what love is
Hot deep-red bloody sopping my mitten
Burrowing into blade art
No pain
No pain

Until I saw his skates
Torn and filthy punching toward me
Only when he genuflected his
Denim knee a mountain to my blood river

Only then did I cry

Drive in to Movie Madness
Twin Drive-In, October 9, 1971, Walker Road and Highway 98

see the big 5 feature dusk to dawn shows at the twin drive-in come early stay late shrieking black and white Windsor Star ads terrified thick-lipped ladies mouths agape as skulls triple stack horrors the naked back of a woman entices as reptile claws wrap around open necks always women always thin nightgown-clad those monsters keep coming back in bloodthirsty lust for human flesh and dollar bills and silver coins and leather seats in this town built on cars the drive-in breathes life into life off the line though neatly lined darts chargers valiants cordobas the chrysler family represents and ford mercury meteors splash starlight wishes over the white of the big screens east and west just take your pick put your hand on the radio dial and connect to heston fonda enter the castle of evil visit hercules in the haunted world lean your seat back as pretty boy floyd flicks shivers up and down your spine grab the popcorn some dogs and suds at the concession stand just don't inhale the chemicals smoking out the mosquitoes suck a cig instead keep your hands warm with a window heater don't think about the looming death of this fine cheap entertainment this post-war projection of economically saavy family friendly or date-night madness of movies at the drive-in

One Love
Emancipation Festival 1940s-50s, Jackson Park, Ouellette Ave

300,000 people
one body
one skin
one love

grandstand gathering for the
greatest freedom show on earth

diana ross sings the pain
meat sizzles on barbecues

pageant contestants strutt their
stuff to 600,000 clapping palms

three times dr. martin luther king
opens his heartsong into the crowds

canada strong and free
open arms made of railroads

for safe passage
for dignity deliverance

it was our park the world held up
it was our street that took the stage

we burned a different fire
held a torch of truth

fueled in the arms of the trees
rooted in universal belonging

where have these stories gusted?
we must bring back their roar

bring forth the riotous revelry of
a past that rose up

300,000 people
one body
one skin
one love

Cluster
In response to: Health Unit Investigates Possible Cancer Cluster in Remington Park, Windsor Star, March 13, 2015 bi-line: Craig Pearson*

A grouping of incidents related like the
Extended family of Death
Cousin Cancer Papa Pesticide Grandma Grief
Family shows up to these reunions
It's a swarming of pollution and power
Politics and poverty
Worst of all it's a genuflect to
Diversion and irresponsibility
Until cancer shows up like that
Wicked uncle everyone
Hopes would stay away
Death keeps his doors open

Metal gets recycled and sifts through the
Choking air onto our streets
Red dust covers the sidewalks like
Death's powder graffiti

Trains idle and annoy
Oil dumps into drains
With lead and manganese and carbon and
Chemical words too long to pronounce

We can all read and say cancer
Death loves it when his family grows and grows
Windsor is a continuous giver

Our lungs breasts colons livers and
Prostates pile up in mountains
Beside the oceans of tears that flow in his backyard

Brothers old and new
Folks just doing their jobs
Others dedicated to change
We cluster together on opposite
Sides of a ragged fault line
The pressure is past pardoning
The system is *fucked*

Are you bringing your picnic basket
To the family reunion lunch in Jackson Park?
My feet are magnetized and no matter
How hard I try I can't stop feeling my
Armpits for lumps and crying alone in my car
When I think about all the death around me
Death's a puppet-master with a strong stage

And we're all on the same team
Hiding our shiny silver investigator badges
Deep in the bowels of our fear
It's not easy to find a trench coat that
Covers all the destruction we see and feel
It's not easy puking from chemo or
Running your hand over the scars
Where your breasts once lived

Man O'War

I never liked the name
I ain't a man and a horse never loved a war
For we all died for the two-legged
Stupidity over sky and land
That can't never be owned

These two-leggeds named me after a war ship
They saw me galloping
Like heavy artillery was trying
To snatch my hooves
Impossible
You can't shoot the wind

Still they watched me
Awed at my flickering speed
My fearless force
Took a leather strap to my mane and
Did their best to tame me

Still they ran me in ovals
My muscles hulked and
My fur shined
Oh and I ran
I ran for them
Cheering me on

But then the Riddle bought me
His determination made my hair tickle
I felt we shared the same fire so
I let him think he was in control

I let him put the small man on my back
And I flew around those tracks
Pounding the dirt like it was a petulant foal

One race became more important than the others
I swooned past Niagara Falls
My eyes revealing a magical water miracle
My equine brain could barely comprehend
I felt the surge of power in those falls and
I vowed to run like the water cascades

To Kenilworth in Windsor we journeyed
The stadium grandstand swollen with gawkers
Come race start ten thousand two-legs stood on their toes
Looking for me and my main competitor Sir Barton
I could tell by the twitch of his rump that I had the race won
But out of the gates I gave him lead for entertainment

My jockey squeezed and choked as I pushed around the bend
In four strides I took him—that mighty-named thoroughbred
Sir Losing Now
If they were listening they would have heard me snort as the lengths settled between us
They would have heard me turn into water rushing over the edge of this cliff called racing

Two years of my life spent running in circles
Twenty wins for twenty-one races
I made people believe that I could be tamed
I was always running
Toward that crashing down of foam and pressure

I made people cheer
I made people rich
I made people poor

And now...
My spirit flows like the hearts of the oceans
In the four-legs that carry my blood
Over more finish lines
Than I could have ever crossed

Now I am free

Tornado

1.
god made a statement
that June 17, 1946
tornado swept city
touched down three times
three strikes
we were out

2.
I care about destruction
I am a violent rotation of air
The air you breathe

                I will break you
                I will break it all

3.
ten minutes of weather power
electric grey cone
that's what they said

first taps on an earth dance floor
smoke air dirt destruction
that's what they said

grinding and breaking till
confused souls dust to a choking heaven

                I will break you
                I will break it all

4.
She was terrified
So I lied and told her it was a game
Run from the gray wind!
We beat the monster!
Ice cream at home!
I screamed as it took her
Saw the fear blow out of her blue-velvet eyes
Saw the life twist out of her 3 year-old body
Felt my legs buckle
My knees bounce
Take me! Take me!
I let it lift me
Devastate my body
Free my soul
Our heaven is ice cream
    I will break you
    I will break it all

5.
Mama will be angry
My clothes are torn and hanging in a tree
A tree that the tower of wind ripped from the earth
We made tornado funnels in science class

Mama will be angry
It's passed dinner hour and I need to set the table
I am cold and need to cover my body

Mama will be angry
All her favourite houses are broken
People are crying and bleeding

She doesn't like a mess
She doesn't like pain

Mama…please don't be angry
Where are you?
Did you find a hiding place?

                      I will break you
                      I will break it all

6.
I cowered beside a cement wall
My fingers bled from holding so tightly
The sound of the swarming belly was devil song

But nothing
Nothing was worse than what my eyes dared see
Monster gray scooped him up
This son of someone riding his bike in the race for his life
Like a wind-handed giant
It took him into the darkness
Spit out the bike

I waited
Hands chaffing
Heart shattering
For his body to return to the ground

I waited
It's sixty years now
I'm waiting for his soul to settle

>   I will break you
>   I will break it all

7.
Dangerous air rogue
Swept me off my feet
I dangled in your wind grip
Bursting grey heat
The baby in my belly
Felt your beat

You dropped us down
Smacked the ground
And we lived
So profound
Another day's worth of breath
Kept us bound

Then nineteen with child
Death took hold
Tornado leaves a story
To be told

>   I will break you
>   I will break it all

8.
god made a statement
that June 17, 1946
tornado swept city
touched down three times
three strikes
we were out

god made a statement
wrote lessons with the blood of children
human pens making marks across a ruined road
what was his message?

a 9-year-old girl
clothes blown off
face muzzled in mud
lay 75 feet from her parents
their skin wrinkled like elephants
aged improperly skin in purples and blues

god made a statement
that June 17, 1946
it screamed in the tongue of a peaceful funnel centre

I am here
In the centre of your pain
I am here
In the core of your destruction
I am here
In the lifting of your material world

                                      I will break you
                                      I will break it all

Some Fine Hands
Walker Farms, January 1894

Susan Diem worked on the Walker farm as a housekeeper, cook and maid. She used a lantern to milk the cows in the morning before the light—she also made butter and bread. She married Fred Dahl, a bricklayer from Woodslee in 1895 and they had 12 children. (article by Elain Weeks)

A man startled me in the
Barn this morning
I was shaking with cold
My lantern's flame throwing
Shadows on the slush-dirty hay but
I had plenty more shake in me for fear

In these dark mornings
It's just the cows and me
But Betty Blue my main mama heifer
She wasn't spooked at all
I took that as a good sign

He was quick to grab my wrist and hold me steady
Before I stumbled and fell and darn near set the barn ablaze
I was flushed with embarrassment and anger
No man had ever touched my wrist

I'm Fred said the man his coveralls
Dirty and torn in the elbows
I didn't mean to scare you

Three hundred cows on this farm and this
Fred fellow had to find me and my Betty Blue

She's the most beautiful he said
Pointing a gnarled finger at Betty Blue
He was quick to fold his hand at his side
Crushed between bricks he told me
I'm Fred from Woodslee
My pop and I lay bricks for the Walkers

I nodded my voice stuck somewhere in my toes
Betty Blue let out a deep mmmmaaawww
Her udders plump and dripping

I need to milk her was all I could manage
As I pulled my stool to her side
The sound of her warm thick milk
Trumming in the tin was music to my ears
Loud enough to cover the sound of
My heart bashing against my ribcage

My cheeks burned again and
No Winter's cold could cool
The heat pushing beneath my skin
Betty Blue nudged Fred's shoulder as
If they were in cahoots

Those are some fine hands Fred said as
He watched me
His words smooth as fresh cream
Made my knees knock and my
Shoulders turn to butter
My fine hands lost their grip and
I shot his mason boots with a
Spray of Betty Blue's freshest

He laughed from his belly
I was liquid with apologies
Betty Blue shuffled in her stanchion
Same time tomorrow then Fred said

For one whole year he met me in the
Romantic darkness of the barn
I baked fresh bread and
Mended his torn coveralls
Bless her bovine heart Betty Blue
Smiled each time she heard his voice

That year she won the Walkers'
Best Milk Award and
Fred asked for my hand
In marriage

I gave him both
Those are some fine hands indeed

The Day the Fire Blazed
Walker Farms, 1937

In 1937 a large storage barn and implement shed in the orchard burned...a crowd came to watch the fire...Camilla Stodgell Wigle of Windsor remembers afternoon excursions in the family carriage to Walker Farms for fresh produce. "We would head up Walker Road, past all the wonderful houses and factories—and then, at last—we'd arrive at the farm; it was wonderful!"—(Article by Elaine Weeks)

Papa promised a trip to Walker Farms that afternoon
I remember my belly singing a hunger song thinking about
The taste of the crunch apples and cold milk
That would keep me smiling till sundown
I wore my favourite flowered skirt and yellow bonnet
Come high noon the centre-blue-sky sun was leading us
In our family carriage toward my favourite place in our growing city

Billy from school told me that the folks at the Great Hall were planning
A holiday jamboree and he was going to make me dance with him, silly boy
We passed the grey houses winding in a circle spilling out farm workers and
The massive factories that my little mind could barely comprehend
Oh, to see this fine city through my childhood eyes

Until that day
That perfect sunny day
When the blue sky pulled in blackness
Thick smoke in swathes so big it looked like
God himself was painting *anger*

As our horses neared the
Walker Farms entrance
My nostrils curled in pain
Barn and shed ablaze

There would be
No biting apples
No sipping milk
Just a crowd of us
Gawking at flames
Dancing a death song

It wasn't the last fire that
Would scourge Walker Farms
But it was the first fire
My young eyes beheld
It was the first time I felt the
Heat of childhood innocence
Charred and the changes and
The challenges to my
Understanding of
What gives a city pause

One Lot—The Voice of What Remains of Walker Farms

Today, all that remains of this once enormous state-of-the-art farm and dairy is a small, neglected lot between two light industrial buildings on Deziel Road. (article by Elaine Weeks)

I'm here
a scraggy remnant of history in rich milk
I'm here
a buried sign of ancestry marking community roots

I'm here
in the ghost-choir serenade of a song of remembrance

I'm here
in the stories of your dying past

Come closer behold what remains
Place your hand on my soil skin
I give you my body

Remember history
tell it honestly
Remember legacy
there is life in solid structure

I sing to you a sweet Deziel road song
Can you hear the lowing of cows?

I am the last lot remaining.

A Mootual Moostake
Sherwood. V Walker, 66 Mich. 568, 33 N.W. 919

Rose the 2nd of Aberlone knew that she was pregnant.
But what was a pregnant cow to do?

Her owner, Mr. Hiram Walker—importer, breeder, grocer
And distiller, offered to sell her to
Mr. Theodore Sherwood—farmer and banker,

For a meager price of five and one half cents per pound on the mutual
Agreement that Aberlone was barren, and therefore, significantly less
valuable.

Upon finding out that the beast was, in fact, with calf,
The terms of the sale became quite a problem, and the
Agreement previously understood went to court.

Mr. Walker changed his sale-price tune
For it was a poor business choice to sell
A perfectly fertile bovine for such a low price,
And Mr. Sherwood was not in agreement at all.

This was a seminal case of law. In July 1887, it was decided
By Allen B. Morse—presiding judge, that the contract
Was voidable on the grounds of mutual mistake,

Reasoning by using the traditional test of the mistake
Relating to the substance of the consideration.
The deal was unstruck. The sale never made.

This was a case made for the history books, and the law books too. Rose the 2nd of Aberlone knew all along, but what was a pregnant cow to do—

But moo?

The Canadian Dream

Nonno left Italy age twenty shining on his high cheekbones. Crossing great seas on giant ships while he smoked cigarettes with men who would become his blood-brothers in the new country. He wanted to start his family in Windsor and followed a grumpy, square-shouldered bear of an aunt who promised his mother she'd take care of him—such promises all part of the dream.

He landed with an excited screech of Via Rail's tracks in the east, scooted across the provinces balancing on sheer will and lust for a freedom he liked the taste of—better than dry dusty old country tradition. Zia-the-bear began the assimilation and his favourite part was watching movies every Friday night with the other men—smoking cigarettes and thinking of silver-screen actor names for his future children.

Nonna came a short time later—one trunk and a heart plump with love, a stirring womb and fingers that could sew like they were God's own. This timid woman a seamstress since age ten kept it all stitched together, kept her mouth closed as she sewed the secrets of their destinies into her wedding gown. She loved him deeper than the oceans they crossed, wider than the edges of the new country that became home.

This dream painted hard work, stern faces, strong arms, nimble fingers. Struggle after struggle with money, language, dwelling and work. They kept the dream alive on their own turf in their own time and the house was purchased, the mortgage paid. One child death and three beautiful daughters each with pieces of the Canadian dream hemmed into their psyches. The sound of saying goodbye

to a homeland that never really fades though the new land
is a beautiful symphony to endure.

Sixty-five years and the dream is still alive in the knotted knuckles of
Nonna's wrinkled hands as she sews and knits, glasses of vino soon to
pucker her lips. Her heart half gone with Nonno in heaven or maybe
not half—it's a dream split in two this widow among her kin in the
house unchanged for 30 years.

When did the dream turn beige? The colours emptying with each day
lived one foot in poverty, the other sending money home to Mama,
an old world away? There are so many cracks in the walls at the top of
the stairs, the shadows of slippered feet blackening the pressed down
carpet, and Nonno's shirts still hang on metal hangers in the wardrobe
in the bathroom beside the drawers filled with old toothbrushes, out-
of-shape bobby-pins and 1950s face cream no one will throw away.

Because I Haven't Lived Here: an outsider's view

John B. Lee

If ever I close my eyes and think about cities sometimes I think about Windsor, and whenever I think about Windsor I realize that mine are the memories and imaginings of an outsider. For me, Windsor has most often been a pass-through town and as I've approached her from the four points of the compass I recall mostly traveling due north with the skyline of Detroit looming as an exotic childhood destination. Through the prism of recall I see a yellow band of industrial smoke woven through and smudging clear blue heavens above the cityscape of America. I see the Ambassador Bridge spanning the river as we cross a flag-marked border going over the water and into the tall-building-shadowed environs of Detroit City on annual shopping sprees before school began in September. I've had fond childhood adventures at Tiger Stadium, the Ford Museum, Greenfield Village, the Olympia Stadium, and the Detroit Race Course my father always having been something of a racehorse enthusiast. And we'd return to Canada coming up out of the tessellated white-walled Detroit-Windsor tunnel into the hops and boiled wheat fragrances of Hiram Walker country. I don't know what it's like for others, but for me there has always been a sense of relief leaving America in my rear view and coming home to the familiars of Canada freshened by Windsor daylight blooming in the city. And arriving there to be greeted by the redolence and flavour of chicken dinners served with fries and coke at the recently closed Tunnel Barbecue.

I've also come from the west traveling east along the blue water highway past Lake St. Clair and her recently gentrified shores entering Riverside. I've come from the east as I travel west into Sandwich by way of Wheatley and Leamington thinking of the double blue sky of Lake Erie and the southernmost point in Canada at Pelee Island. But mostly I've come via the 401 Highway traveling through the lakebed flatlands of Kent and Elgin. From there I've turned north by way of Walker Road heading for my friend Marty Gervais' house on Bynng, passing by factories, past airport road, puzzling over the frequency of French names given her streets and wondering how one might say the word for the Belgian town Ypers, and also wondering why so many battles seem to have given this region of town its identifiers. For their part Canadian veterans of the First World War pronounced it "Wipers" as in—windshield wipers. And as we all learned by rote the poem "In Flanders Fields," we might also know that John McCrae wrote that poem during the second battle of Ypres.

But as I think of Windsor my strongest childhood recollection involves radio station CKLW. In its prime CKLW had the eighth largest listening audience in North America. CKLW gave teenagers of the sixties their first taste of Motown music, the Beatles, the British invasion, and Rock and Roll writ large by the Big 8. If I close my eyes I'm once again the boy in his bedroom on the farm lying in the country gloaming with my radio tuned to Windsor, Ontario, Canada falling asleep to the sound of the summer of 1968 and Paul McCartney singing "Hey Jude" as the evening faded into dream.

And I also remember the night I received the inaugural Black Moss Press "Souwesto Award" in Elias Deli on Ouellette Avenue. A breakfast destination for the people who worked in the heart of the downtown, Elias Sleiman would walk from table to table greeting the police officers, detectives, lawyers, journalists, writers, and judges who dined there just after the sunup hours of morning. Now closed it remains in the memory as a sad reminder of the losses we feel when landmarks pass into history. If ever I close my eyes and think of the city, I think of the city residing within. That is the one where we live when we write. We write of the city as we think of the music we've heard and we listen for faint traces of melody wrung deep in the soul as we break into song.